Our Literary Travels

Walter Cummins
&
Thomas E. Kennedy

Our Literary Travels

Our Literary Travels

Published by Serving House Books

Copenhagen, Denmark and South Orange, NJ

www.servinghousebooks.com

ISBN: 978-1-947175-23-5

Library of Congress Control Number: 2020934129

Member of The Independent Book Publishers Association

First Serving House Books Edition 2020

Cover Concept: Alison Cummins

Serving House Books Logo: Barry Lereng Wilmont

Unless otherwise indicated, all travel photographs in these essays were taken by the authors. Some historical photographs were found in the Internet.

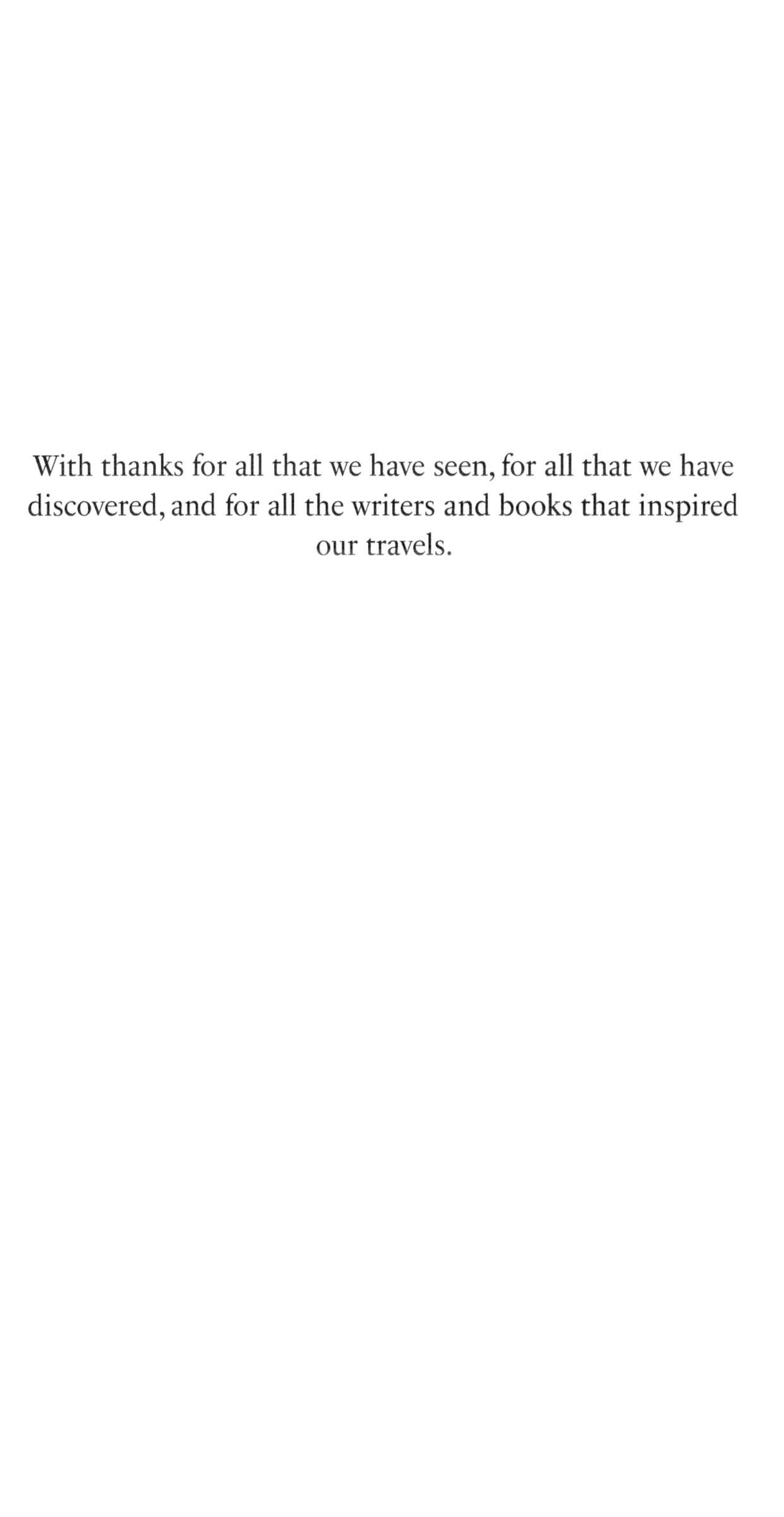

With thanks for all that we have seen, for all that we have discovered, and for all the writers and books that inspired our travels.

CONTENTS

WHAT WE'VE SEEN

Castles, moats, canals, bullet holes, prisons, lions, pump rooms, slave quarters, bookshelves, erotic ceilings, resistance fighters, ferries, churches, hotels, oil paintings, cigars, wall art, pubs, tombstones, yachts, airports, taxis, bush tents, and undergrowth.

In the footsteps of Jane Austen, Ernest Hemingway, Fyodor Dostoevsky, James Boswell and Samuel Johnson, Charles Dickens, Virginia Woolf, George Bernard Shaw, William Butler Yeats, Knut Hamsun, Halldór Laxness, Giovanni Boccaccio, William S. Burroughs, Georges Rodenbach, Heinrich Böll, Hyam Plutzik, Franz Kafka, and many others.

We began our literary travels many decades ago but did not come up with the concept of writing about them until we were part of a gathering of American and Canadian expatriates at a bar in the Place de la Contrescape on Paris' Left Bank in the summer of 2001. Many photographs were taken, and Tom described the event.

That piece initiated an online series on Web Del Sol, first called The Literary Traveler, then changed to The Literary Explorer after a legal threat from the lawyer for a commercial site that had trademarked the term—unbeknownst to us. This renaming took place after our first group of essays and photographs had been published under *The Literary Traveler* title in 2005. Whatever our adventures were called—travels or explorations—we kept going, seeking the literary connections whenever we found ourselves in a new destination. Fortunately, for us there are few, if any, places on the planet that don't enjoy a literary connection. As many as we have seen between us, we've barely made a dent in the possibilities.

This collection is a sampling of all that is out there and, we hope, an inspiration for readers to pack their own suitcases and head off for their own literary discoveries.

MIAMI DAYS
Poetry, Stella, Art, Fois Gras, Ale, Cigars, Books & Books & The Betsy

Thomas E. Kennedy

> Out of my life I fashioned a fistful of words
> When I opened my hand, they flew away.
> —Hyam Plutzik

I. THE BETSY AND THE POET

I am not familiar with the poetry of Hyam Plutzik before I begin my week in residence in The Writer's Room at The Betsy, a luxurious hotel on Ocean Drive in South Miami Beach (TheBetsyHotel.com).

After I check in and locate my room on the ground floor, the door amid a gallery of Bob Bonis photographs of the Beatles and Rolling Stones on their 1960s tours, I find on the desk, along with a letter of welcome on gold-bordered vellum, a copy of Hyam Plutzik's *Apples from Shinar,* reprinted by Wesleyan University Press from the 1959 edition on the centennial of the poet's birthday. A gift. With an afterword by Yale literary scholar David Scott Kastan.

Hyam Plutzik, I learn, was a name included among the great mid-century American poets—Theodore Roethke, Richard Eberhart, Howard Nemerov,

Elizabeth Bishop, Robert Lowell, Randall Jarrell, Robert Penn Warren, Delmore Schwartz, William Stafford… However, Plutzik died young, at fifty, shortly after being a finalist for the 1961 Pulitzer. The nomination was for *Horatio*, a book-length poem about Hamlet's friend, attempting to absent himself from felicity for the rest of his life to tell Hamlet's story aright.

Moreover, the book is resting on the desk at which Plutzik wrote his poems, taken from the basement of his home in Rochester, New York, where he was a professor at the University. Alongside the Plutzik collection is a sturdy envelope addressed to me with a DVD—*Hyam Plutzik, American Poet*—as well as, beside it, a copy of Harold Robbins' *The Betsy*. There is a self-ironic sense of humor at play here. Flanking the desk are two tall bookcases containing, inter alia, volumes by Hayden Carruth, Sylvia Plath, Ted Hughes, James Tate, an Ann Charters book of photos and biography of the Beats… (Every room in The Betsy includes a shelf of ten or twelve books.) Also on the desk is The Betsy newsletter with a color picture of myself and a bio note under the words "In Residence in The Writer's Room…" and a bookmark, embedded with wildflower seeds: "Use it to mark your place or moisten it thoroughly, plant it in soil, and watch the wildflowers bloom." On the obverse are printed the Plutzik lines,

> The abrupt appearance of a yellow flower
> Out of the perfect nothing, is miraculous.

Hanging on the luxurious walls of the room are framed Plutzik lines. The letter of greeting tells me I am welcome to help myself to the minibar, to the snacks, to dine in the hotel restaurants, to drink in the lounge, to enjoy the hotel's outdoor pool, or the white sand beach just across the street . I have seldom in my life felt quite so welcome. The letter is signed by the hotel chairman, the general manager, and the vice president for philanthropy, the former the third child of Plutzik, Jonathan, the latter the fourth daughter, Deborah.

I consider watching the DVD, but it is past 10 pm, and I would like to catch the rooftop lounge before I sleep. On the roof, across Ocean Drive from the Atlantic, I sit at a table, gazing out onto the dark ocean night and a dented orange moon in the velvet sky, a chill bottle of Stella Artois at my elbow, breeze off the ocean drying the sweat on my face, and leaf through *Apples from Shinar.*

Before I rode the elevator four floors to this roof, I quickly googled at the hotel desk computer (also at my disposal) "Shinar," because I hadn't a clue: Shinar was a biblical location in Mesopotamia, perhaps from the Hebrew for two rivers or two cities: the Tigris and Euphrates, or Uruk and Babylon.

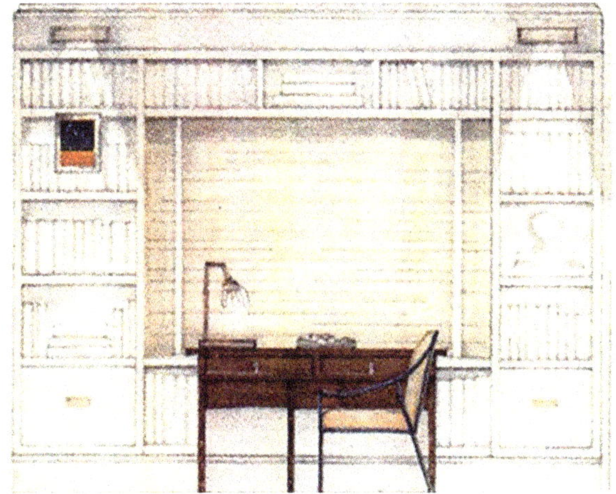

There's no title poem in the book to give a hint. The hint must be in the title itself. Perhaps we're talking the birth of civilization here. Gilgamesh and Uruk. Shinar also enclosed the plain that became the Tower of Babel, so we're also talking language and communication and the failure to communicate, too. Or maybe we're talking Eden, the forbidden fruit? Apples is plural, however—maybe apples stand for the poems themselves, the fruit of willfulness, awareness, self-consciousness, the will of human beings, the naming of things?

The young woman behind the bar comes over to my chair on the lip of paradise and asks if I'd like another Stella. If her name is Eve, Eva, or Evelyn, I think, I'll bite her, but she might not understand, so I simply say, "Yes, thank you." I read the Afterword by David Scott Kaplan first: "In the 1950s Plutzik was clearly recognized as among the generation of poets claiming the mantle of Frost and Jeffers, Stevens and MacLeish."

Louis Untermeyer and Stanley Kunitz served as the jurors for the 1961 Pulitzer, but it seems that Plutzik was also short-listed in 1950 and '60, too. Ted Hughes spoke of Plutzik's visions as "authentic and piercing, and the song in them is strange – dense and harrowing, with unforgettable tones. The best of his work seems to me marvelously achieved, a sacred book." Born in Brooklyn in 1911 to recent immigrants from Belarus who soon moved to a farm near Bristol, Connecticut, Plutzik won Yale's highest award for poetry in 1933 and again in 1941, the only person ever to win twice. He also won the Yale Younger Poets Award in 1940.

I remind myself, here on the roof beneath the dented orange moon, that I am reading secondary opinions and facts. Go to the poems themselves:

> As the great horse rots on the hill...
> till the stars wink through his skull;
> As the stars become husk and radiance...
> Thus you prepare the future for me and my loved ones.

And,

> Trying to imagine a poem of the future,

I saw a nameless jewel lying
Lurid on a table of black velvet...
Then one said: "I am the poet of the damned.
My eyes are seared with the darkness that you willed me.
This jewel is my heart, which I no longer need."

And,

a great stag came out of the woods,
Broad-antlered, approaching slowly on the moonlit field,
And looked around him like a king and re-
entered the dark.

By one a.m., I am sated with eating poetry and sipping Stella, am in bed, eyes closed to the great flat screen at the foot of the bed, dropping off to the babbling nonsense of Fox News.

II. THE VIEW AND THE EXAM

Today, I am dining with my hosts in north Miami—the woman who organized my stay at The Betsy: the writer Jessie Aufiery and her husband Walter, from Paris, and their twin daughters, 11-year-old Chloe and Mira, and Jessie's father, the painter Dennis Aufiery and his wife Carol. Jessie and Walter and their daughters had lived in Paris for the past many years, before that in Manhattan.

Jessie picks me up at The Betsy and drives north over the bridge across Biscayne Bay to their 79th Street high-rise. The apartment is comfortably sized, but leads onto a broad balcony with an astonishing view. The photograph that I have does not do it justice. It includes Biscayne Bay and the bridge and, further to the south, the Atlantic ocean—a dizzying, glittering expanse of sea. Literally I cannot take my eyes off it.

Jessie's husband Walter is a tall, slender man of about forty and offers fois gras at the table on the balcony with a glass of red which could only have been chosen by a Frenchman. Nibbling goose liver and sipping burgundy, trying not to be hypnotized by the view, I remind Chloe and Mira that they have promised to show me their sketchbooks. They have just been admitted into a school that runs from sixth grade to twelfth for gifted students of art. The entrance exam consisted simply of their sketching for about an hour; after fifteen minutes they were admitted.

View of Biscayne Bay and other waters from Jessie & Walter's balcony

They show their sketches, first the one, then the other: the one not showing touches the shoulder of the one showing, their spirits clearly connected. Their sketchbooks are definitely influenced by their artist grandfather, Dennis Aufiery—studies in still lifes, gradation of shadings, sketches of hands, faces... The girls' slender faces contain the direct, steady gaze of artists.

Suddenly it occurs to me that this talent, unlike the tendency to conceive twins, would not likely skip a generation. I've always thought of Jessie as primarily a writer since the first time I met her—when, as judge of a short fiction competition, I picked her story for top prize. (It was good that I didn't see how beautiful she was before I picked—this way, I could honestly say I hadn't even seen her before she won!)

Now, I ask, "Jessie, do you paint

as well?"

"Not really," she says, but reluctantly produces a portrait of her father that is excellently rendered—his squared jaw, his nose, the blue of his eyes.

"That portrait is good, I think," Dennis says and then asks, "Say, do you know which ankle bone is higher? Right or left side? Don't look now!"

I didn't even realize that we had two ankle bones on each ankle, but it makes sense. Whatever it is, it turns out I'm wrong, and he asks, "How many times can the length of your foot fit up your calf?" And, "How many times will the length of your hand fit up your forearm?"

Wrong every time, but it comforts me to know that there is this unapparent symmetry to human anatomy. It also comforts me to know that a writer doesn't have to know that symmetry—all a writer has to know is that an artist has to know it.

As we come in from the balcony to dinner, I notice that there areour framed 6" x 9" oil paintings ranged along the sofa, propped up face out against the back.

"Pick the one you want," Dennis says.

Although I never met him before, he knows that I have long admired his art.

"You don't have to pick now," he says. "You can eat first and think about it."

But I know that if I have much more wine, I will not be fit to pick. From my place at the dinner table, enjoying beef bourguignon and more burgundy, I can see the four paintings on the sofa and glance up from time to time, sensing that it's an examination: what I pick is what I deserve.

A few hours later, again out on the balcony, I notice it is nearing midnight. Some of these people have to work tomorrow. Dennis has gone to bed. Carol is still up, as are Jessie and Walter. Chloe and Mira have hugged me goodnight, warming my heart. Carol is reading one of my books, but exhorts me not to tell her the ending. "Is it happy?" she asks. "Don't tell me, don't tell me!"

"I really have to get back to the hotel," I say. Jessie phones a taxi, and I decide that when I go into the living room, I will pick the painting Zen style: just quickly pick. Before the sofa, my eye goes first to the one on the far right, then bounces to the far left, and I pick that one. Holding it, I hear Carol and Jessie call out in unison, "You picked the best!"

Oil painting by Dennis Aufiery

(Now, as I sit on my red sofa in my tiny living room in Copenhagen, I look across to the painting, its red impressionist lighthouse, across a choppy aqua and black with dashes of coral strait, beneath a sky of patchwork color, over a colorist jut of earth, I agree. I chose the best. I passed the exam. The painting fits in among the dozen colorist paintings and lithographs on my wall.)

III. BOOKS & BOOKS AND WYNWOOD WALLS

Last night I did my reading at Books and Books in Coral Gables, a fine experience in an expansive bookstore of squared wings around a courtyard bar which we end seated in over several glasses of wine. The book store live-streamed the reading, and it can be viewed on new.livestream.com/uainmedia/thomas-kennedy and copies of my back titles were ordered for the event. Afterwards I signed many copies of *Kerrigan in Copenhagen*, and they will be distributed to the various Books & Books shops. Margie, the mother of my friend and colleague, novelist David Grand, attended the reading with David's stepdad, Joel. Margie is a lovely woman. She came from Middle Village, Queens, where I had a girlfriend in 1964. Did she know Dry Harbor Road? She did.

I take advantage of the opportunity to give Dennis a copy of the new novel I am reading from, *Kerrigan in Copenhagen*, as a token of thanks for his painting. A couple who came to the reading and joined us for drinks, the poet Letisia Cruz and the fiction writer Bob Beaird, suggest that my stay in Miami must include a visit to Wynwood.

Jessie collects me in her Audi late next morning, and we follow the directions of her GPS tracking device north to Wynwood. She explains that Wynwood was previously a slum but the artists have moved in and, as will happen, mounting real estate prices and gentrification followed them. It is still not quite gentrified, however.

When the massive, low walls of the buildings on the broad roadways and streets suddenly are adorned with ornate graffiti, I realize we are there. Graffitti is not the word; these are composed and breathtaking, giant figures amidst intricate geometrical designs of colored spectrums.

Our first stop is the Wynwood Kitchen and Bar (wynwoodkitchenandbar.com) on NW 2nd Avenue, where we meet Letisia and Bob. Letisia, she says, is reading my novel, and over the first, very spicy bloody Mary, she says, "I have to know, is the ending happy?"

"I don't want to spoil it for you."

"I have to know if it's happy, that's all. Not details."

"Sort of."

Letisia fits well into Wynwood. The whole length of her arms, including the shoulders and upper back, are decorated with tattoos: On the right arm is a girl holding a bluebird in her hand; her body grows out of a dandelion, and she is wearing a purple dress, her black hair, adorned with a red rose, metamorphosing into birds (that part is on Letisia's shoulder and upper back, visible above her tank top). A flower is inked on her left wrist, another flower on her forearm, both red, and a small bow and arrow decorates the inside of her upper arm.

Born in Cuba, Letisia moved to the U.S. as a baby. Bob is of Mexican descent but grew up in Michigan. When they first met, Letisia teased him, asking, "What's with this 'Bob,' Roberto?" But his real name is Robert, and he's called Bob and speaks standard Midwestern. After thirty years in Copenhagen, I have more of a foreign accent than Letisia, who speaks flawless American as well as flawless, as far as I can tell, Spanish.

From left, Jessie Aufiery, Thomas E. Kennedy (author), Letisia Cruz in front of Wynwood Wall. Author cannot deny resemblance to Tony Clifton. (Art by Stelios Faitkas of Greece; photo by Bob Beaird)

After a few spicy bloody Marys and a brunch of questo frito, medjool dates, pork belly and some kind of spiced spinach on the back patio of the restaurant, surrounded by walls of art of Logan Hicks, Ron English, Ryan McGiness and many others, including a large graphic shark mouth by Kenny Scharf, we stroll alongside, among the Wynwood Walls (thewynwoodwalls.com).

Bob snaps a photo of me flanked by Jessie and Letisia in front of the first mural, a huge blond woman in skimpy underwear, lofting a phallic missile. The women in the photo look delightful; however, I look rather like Tony Clifton, Jim Carrey's decidedly unpleasant, Vegas crooner alter ego as Andy Kaufmann in Man on the Moon. There are many other photos of huge murals on the Wynwood Walls and outside – a woman touching her lips and one, smaller one (visible only at certain angles) looking through her interlaced fingers (by the Australian artist Rone), a sixty-foot-long Lost Lover with a central golden figure (by the artist Faith47), another of a woman floating colorful images 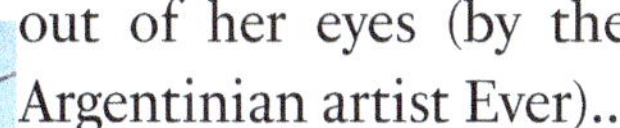
out of her eyes (by the Argentinian artist Ever)...

We stop in Panther Coffee (panthercoffee.com) for refeshments of cake and strong beer, the Wynwood Cigar factory on NW 24th St.—it, too, has murals—where I purchase three Edgar Hoill robustos, two to be shared by Bob and Letisia and Jessie and myself, one to be sent home with Jessie for Dennis Aufiery, who kindly provided me with a Cohiba the night before.

We end the day passing robustos and drinking half-quart cans of Dale's Pale Ale at the back of Lester's on NW 2nd Ave (Lestersmiami.com), and we have one of the best conversations of my life—if only I could remember it...

At one point, Jessie must have driven me back to The Betsy because I find myself atop the rooftop, sitting in a chair at a table against the rear wall. The moon above me is no longer dented – it is full and bright, orange as a cat's eye regarding me, and I am sipping a Stella and reading lines of Plutzik by its light:

> If these lesser things are subsumed within the Good—
> These corrupt shapes: desk, mirror or tree –
> The falsely transliterated, strangely planed
> Creatures of eyesight and the sentient bones
> (Themselves in the web of the spider), then all times
> Are poses of the one actor, Time...
> And still it is hot noon on the sea Tethys
> Where the protoplasmic slime begets Aphrodite
> Whose belly is history till the moon falls...

IV. THE PEN AND THE FILM

My last day at The Betsy is bright with sun and a pure blue sky, and I decide to take a chaise lounge on the beach and jot notes of my visit. Clipped to my shirt pocket is my Montblanc, the ballpoint with which I've written the first draft of the most recent dozen of my books. The young woman in the beach shed provides a large white towel, and the young man hurries out to set up a chaise lounge for me, covered with a fitted terry cloth sheet.

It is hot beneath the yellow sun, and I take off my shirt and toss it on the lounge to wade out and dive into the aqua blue water of the Atlantic. The water is womb warm, and I swim until my muscles are agreeably weary and my hunger has been stoked to visions of shrimp cocktail on the rooftop with a Stella Artois in which to swim the crustaceans.

I thank and tip the young man and young woman. By the time I cross the road to The Betsy my swim trunks are already dry, and I ride directly up to the rooftop, order a Stella and shrimp big as large crayfish. And while I wait I think to jot a note and reach to my shirt pocket for my Montblanc where I always carry it. It is not there.

Aside from the value of the pen (it cost $350), it sat with such balance in my hand, awaiting the inspiration of language, and I am attached enough to it that I am blinded with anxiety at its loss, even while trying to reason that it's only a thing. But it is truly a *cherished* thing!

Calling to the barmaid that I will be back and to watch my things, I ride the elevator to the lobby and jog across the road to the pathway that leads to the beach, my sandals flopping beneath my feet.

"Did you see a black Ballpoint pen?" I ask at the beach hut, trying to quell the panic in my voice.

The young woman smiles. "You want pen?" she asks, handing me a disposable gray plastic ballpoint.

I dash down to the chaise lounge I used and search the creases and folds of the mattress, but it is not there. I stand disconsolately on the beach, as unhappy as if I'd just lost my passport, my wallet, unhappy as if I'd just lost my identity. I truly *valued* that pen.

Out of the corner of my eye in the white sand, I glimpse a speck of familiar shiny black and jump for it. About to be swallowed forever by the hot, white sand is my Montblanc!

Looking around for someone to whom to explain how happy I am, how elated with relief, I realize that this is a moment I cannot share with anyone. Who will understand, who can understand? I am alone with this elation.

The last act of my day, I decide, will be to watch in my room the 2006 film about Hyam Plutzik—*Hyam Plutzik, American Poet*, produced and co-directed by the Academy Award nominated Christine Choy with her daughter Ku-long Siegel. Literary advisor to the film was Ed Moran. I fit it into the DVD player and have a cold Stella at hand, my Montblanc with which to take notes.

Many of the things I have noted in this essay are related in the film, many lines from Plutzik poems are read by Donald Hall, by Hayden Carruth, Stanley Kunitz, Galway Kinnell, and by Plutzik himself (he sounded rather like Lawrence Ferlinghetti—or should I say that Ferlinghetti sounded rather like Plutzik?)

But the film also tells how Plutzik went into World War II, into the Army Air Corps, in 1942 and served until the end of the war, how he wrote a poem about the ten crew members lost in an American bomber that was shot down, how he wrote a poem entitled "Hiroshima." The film tells about how his first language was Yiddish, about his determination to be a poet, about his determination to "merit the respect of intelligent men." It also tells about how he took on the "conventional" anti-Semitism of T. S. Eliot in "For T.S.E. Only," and how unpopular that was in those days, in that place, how accepted was the anti-Semitism of Hemingway and Eliot and Pound and their peers. He did so compellingly, without embarrassment, implored "brother Thomas..." "Thomas, Thomas" to "weep together for our exile," ending, "You hypocrite lecteur! Mon semblable! Mon frère!" And this was in upstate New York, a bastion of Republicanism, supportive of the Army McCarthy hearings.

The film also tells about his family—his children, his sons Jonathan and Alan, his daughters Roberta Plutzik Baldwin and Deborah Plutzik Briggs. And especially about his wife, Tanya.

She relates how in the few years before his death, on January 8th, 1962, he was becoming more known and how she listens to recordings of her husband reading his poems: "That's one of the most important pleasures I have." About how, although he served his country during World War II, he would surely have been opposed to Vietnam.

But most remarkable is the way the film ends. Tanya Plutzik has been reluctant throughout the filming to allow the filmmaker into Hyam's study in the basement, but she finally consents. It is a modest place, a few bookshelves, a small window at the top edge of the basement wall.

The camera makes a round of the study, and then Tanya says, "I'm done. Are you done?" And the brief remainder of the film shows her from the back, slowly climbing the basement stairs, while her husband recites:

Of light, the torment of beauty deep in the throat
And strive in secret, this brotherhood so small,
To climb the stairway out of the dust a moment
Before the lying down to sleep and the surrender.

Author's Note: Unless otherwise indicated all photographs are by Jessie Vail Aufiery—the hotel art was kindly provided by the Hotel Betsy and the book cover is from the original 1959 edition.

TINKER BELL AND EVERY IMAGINABLE COMFORT
Prague Post-Kafka

Walter Cummins

While the notion of exploring Prague had intrigued my wife, Alison, and me for years, we decided to give our visit a focus with the goal of exploring the Franz Kafka legacy. But, much to our surprise, we discovered Walt Disney too.

From the day we arrived in Prague and saw the twin spires of the Kyn church behind the Old Town square, we found influences on Disney at every turn, a cartoon world emerging from the architecture of his heritage. I had arrived to seek auras of Kafka—where he had lived and worked, where he was buried—but kept blurring Franz with Walt; in fact, getting a stronger sense of a Disneyfied reality than of the dark settings that haunted Joseph K.

It turns out that confusion isn't unique. A web site called

futurecasts.com notes: "Prague is a thoroughly charming city, with pervasive idiosyncratic architectural flourishes added to the facades and roofs. These make it look like a set from a Walt Disney animated film. Tinker Bell might have flown in over the rooftops at any minute." Some lament the transformation of a city minimally untouched by the two world wars and Communist invasion into a twenty first-century tourist haven. The chief European correspondent of *Washington Times*, Gareth Harding, in an article called "Prague Blighted by Tacky Tourism," writes:

> The city has also become more of a fun place to live and visit as hundreds of bars, restaurants and night-clubs have sprouted up and opening hours have been extended. The flipside is that the center of Prague has lost much of the atmosphere which once made it unique. The smoky bars serving up plates of gristly meat and dumplings are gradually being replaced by brighter, trendier, pricier places offering pasta, pizza and pitas. The street markets selling wild mushrooms and garden-produced vegetables have been turned into tourist stalls hawking mass-produced souvenirs. Even the recently-opened Museum of Communism is nestled between a McDonald's burger joint and an Austrian-owned casino. If ever there was a symbol of Prague on the eve of the Czech Republic's entry into the European Union, this is it.

Despite Harding's upset, today's Prague is a very pleasant place—attractive, charming, inviting—even with the packs of tourists that cross the Charles Bridge and climb the steep steps of the Hradny Castle. (Like the castle described in Kafka's novel of that title, "It was neither an old stronghold nor a new mansion, but a rambling pile consisting of innumerable small buildings closely packed together and of one or two storeys; if K. had not known that it was a castle he might have taken it for a little town"—Muir translation). The Old Town Square is spacious and open, al fresco dining tables lining two sides, clusters of camera-ready people waiting for the clock in the tower of the old town hall to chime while mechanical figures perform their centuries-old ritual. Yes, the city is Disneyfied, spruced up, sandblasted, repainted, an architectural museum, destination of tourists from throughout Europe and the world.

Kafka created a make-believe Amerika in his novel of that name, but his vision has no legacy. Disney can be considered responsible for transforming much of the American imagination with his movies and his theme parks, the fantasy land that serves as America's substitute for a mythology, his Mickey Mouse the country's most famous icon. For readers, Kafka's most likely icon is the insect incarnation of Gregor Samsa. But Gregor's Prague no longer exists.

Like the bright-colored Disney animations that expurgate the painful endings of their folk-tale originals, the gray, Nazi-occupied Prague of World War II has been transformed into a bright, happy place, filled with music and cheer.

Kafka wouldn't recognize his city, beyond the shapes of certain familiar buildings. The city depicted in *The Trial* is claustrophobic—tiny rooms, low ceilings, narrow streets, strangers peering in windows.

Oppressive and menacing. Today's Prague is hospitable, filled with art, music—opera, string quarters, jazz– food, pilsner beer, boat rides on the Vltava, a fringe arts festival, shopping streets of shops for the wealthy. No wonder people flock there.

One symbol of the transformation from the Samsa reality to the new Prague can be seen in the location of the InterContinental Hotel at 43/5 Námestí Curieových, the exact site of the building where Kafka in a third-floor room wrote "Metamorphosis." Instead of Gregor's broken family, reduced to sharing their small space with lodgers, affluent tourists luxuriate in plush rooms and dine elegantly in a rooftop restaurant. According to its web site, "The InterContinental's 372 guestrooms, including 89 Suites, have all been recently renovated and feature every imaginable comfort. The hotel offers spacious health club with unique swimming pool, sauna, Jacuzzi, gym and massage facilities as well as most modern golf simulator." Imagine the look on the face of any guest who opened a door and encountered a man-sized bug halfway up a wall, an embedded apple festering in its back.

It's not that Prague wishes to conceal the memory of Kafka like a shameful son left to die in a sealed room and become a "thing" gotten rid of by a charwoman. Instead, like Gregor's sister, Grete, who with "increasing vivacity . . . bloomed into a pretty girl," the city has allowed Kafka's legacy to flourish. In fact, it flaunts him. There is a Kafka Café, a Kafka book store, Kafka tee shirts, a larger than life, a bust on the site of his birthplace at U Radnice 5, even a discrete sign directing visitors to his grave in the New Jewish Cemetery. A 12-foot-high bronze Kafka statue by Czech artist Jaroslav Rona—Kafka sitting on the shoulders of a headless figure—stands in a tiny park between the Spanish Synagogue and the Church of the Holy Spirit. The small building that replaced the birthplace serves as a Kafka museum. As explained by David Sturm, who put together the route of a Kafka walking tour, "Paying the 20-crown entrance fee (about 50 cents) you can view permanent exhibits including photos of Kafka and his family, artifacts of Jewish life in Prague, a map of Kafka-related sites and a timeline of his life. Most interesting is a display of first editions, in-

cluding a 1916 edition of *Metamorphosis*, one of the few of his books published in his lifetime. A counter in the museum will sell you books on Kafka, a bust of his head or coffee mug on which the writer's gaunt face stares intently back at you."

While not actually following Sturm's suggested path, with a list of addresses and a city map, we managed to get to all the Kafka sites over several days. The building that housed the Worker's Accident Insurance Company of the Kingdom of Bohemia at Na Porici 7, where he worked from 1908 to 1922, is now the Hotel Mercure. For a time he lived with his sister Ottla in the small cottage at 22 Golden Lane on the grounds of the Castle, not far from St. Vitus Cathedral. That cottage is now one of a row of shops that require a ticket to visit, with another Kafka café at next door at 23. He also lived just a few buildings away from the astronomical clock near the Old Town Square.

When Franz was a child the family lived on Celetna, an old street leading to the square, at both numbers 2 and 3, the latter for almost a decade. Franz's father, Hermann, the addressee of the famous accusatory letter, ran a fancy goods shop on the lower level of number 3. When we saw it, number 2 was undergoing renovation, a chute projecting into the street, its barricaded front plastered with advertising posters. With Franz's schools and the various apartments of the peripatetic family, the Old Town is chock full of places that could bear the plaque "Kafka slept here."

We even chanced upon an English-language dramatization of "Metamorphosis" in a—for us—hard to find theatre on an obscure street of the Mala Strana district across the Vltava from the central city. We probably weren't the only ones challenged by the location because only a handful of an audience attended that afternoon performance. But it was well worth being lost, retracing our way back from a dead end on a muddy path, constantly referring to the map. The play combined live acting confined to Gregor's room—mainly the contortions of a remarkably acrobatic man in insect-marked tights and two women who made brief pantomime appearances wearing masks—with the projections of grainy black and white movie scenes of the happenings outside Gregor's room. We had expected a curiosity. Instead, the production moved and disturbed. Perhaps the Joseph K difficulty of getting there was essential to the emotional experience.

In a misapprehension, I had assumed Kafka was buried in the Old Jewish Cemetery. But that burial ground, filled to the brim, layer upon layer of close to 100,000 bodies, had been long closed when Kafka died in 1934. It had been in use from 1439 to 1787, Jews forbidden interment outside the ghetto. Kafka actually lies in the family plot in the new Jewish cemetery, established in 1891, at the corner of two rows, just inside a boundary wall, entombed with his father and his sister, across from a plaque honoring Max Brod, his lifelong friend, who disobeyed Franz's dying wishes and, to the glory of twentieth-century literature, refused to burn the then unpublished manuscripts, saving them from the Nazis in 1939 when he fled to Tel Aviv. The new cemetery is a pleasant place, considering its purpose, spread out over acres, lush with green trees and green vines that climb their trunks and blanket the ground.

It's the Old Jewish Cemetery that of all sites in Prague feels the most Kafkaesque, with its centuries of dead piled twelve-deep in caskets one atop the other, the brown headstones jammed into tight spaces and tumbled every which way. During Kafka's lifetime, the streets of the Jewish quarter replicated the oppressiveness: dark, narrow and winding, a suffocating maze. He wrote of this ghetto, "In us all it still lives—the dark corners, the secret alleys, the shuttered windows, the squalid courtyards, the rowdy pubs, the sinister inns." Yet, even in his lifetime, in fact, before he reached his teens, the city had begun a program of urban renewal to widen the streets and improve sanitation. Still, those vanished streets permeate his writing, like the settings of Dickens' London and Dostoevsky's St. Petersburg.

Kafka's characters are trapped in the mysterious tangle of this presence, its blind alleys of ambiguity, its haunting unknowns. Years ago, on the centenary of Kafka's birth in 1983, a year before the 1984 prophesized by George Orwell, I had occasion to compare the world of the two authors:

> Kafka's centenary year, 1983, may be a more significant touchstone of our time than the 1984 of Orwell's dark prophecy. While post-war Western society has measured its political well-being against the potential coming of Big Brother, the literature of the past half century has found its threat to lie inward. Whatever lurks out there is a vast unknown, unnameable; and so, in a world bereft of answers, we have nowhere to turn but within. [. . .] the inner world explored does not yield the rich abundance of Joycean stream-of-consciousness, but rather the wasteland of Kafka's bleak and haunted souls, people with barely remembered pasts, haunted presents, and doubtful futures.
>
> Through sparse sentences, in sparse claustrophobic settings, isolated, alone, denied communication, these barely named figures grope for meaning without a history to inform them or a culture to sustain them. Clues lead them into literal blind alleys; intellect knots them in conundrums. They are not Winston Smiths fearing totalitarian mind control and a manipulated, imprisoning language. No television cameras need probe their little rooms. Their guilts and anxieties are open secrets. No ministry must contrive doublespeak. Though all the resources of language are available to them, meaning is inaccessible . . .
>
> Ultimately, Kafka's world is a more terrifying one than Orwell's. In *1984*, we know our enemies—sinister technology, thought police, the rat in the cage that breaks our wills. An awful power wants to turn us into mindless automata. But in Kafka, not even sure there is an enemy, we are the rat in the cage; we cannot escape into mindlessness, but are condemned to gnaw at our own hearts, brains, and livers.

After seeing Prague, I'd like to revise that conclusion. *The Trial* can be read as prophetic of a historical reality, the fate of the city's Jews under the Nazis. The Old Jewish Cemetery is part of what is called the city's Jewish Museum, not a single building, but a collection of synagogues and sites over several blocks of the old ghetto. To get to the cemetery, you have to pass through the Pincus Synagogue, an empty building whose white walls are covered with the alphabetically listed names of the Czech Jewish Holocaust victims. In a side room are displayed heartbreaking drawings by children in the death camp of Terezin, marvelously imaginative creations from small hands soon to face extermination.

They and their parents and their families—the names inscribed on the walls—actualized Joseph K's fictional indictment, the knock on the door in the morning, the accusation against which he cannot defend himself. Unlike Joseph K, they knew their "crime"—racial identity—but as with Joseph K, their assassins wanted them to die "like a dog." Yet they are named on a wall, commemorated, haunting us with their humanity.

Of course, once you step out from the Pincus Synagogue and walk the few blocks back to the Old Town Square, you're in a different time and a different place, much more likely to see Tinker Bell floating over the spires than Storm Troopers goose-stepping down the cobblestones.

ALFIE, ELEPHANT GRASS, AND A JAGUAR
A Visit to the West of Ireland for the Kenny-Naughton Festival

Thomas E. Kennedy

> "'...she wanted me to go for a trip to the West of Ireland, and I said I wouldn't,' said Gabriel moodily. 'O, do go, Gabriel,' [his wife] cried. 'I'd love to see Galway again.' 'You can go if you like,' said Gabriel coldly."
>
> —James Joyce, "The Dead"

In "The Dead," Gabriel Conroy is accused of being a "West Brit" because he is more interested in European culture than the original culture of Ireland, specifically of western Ireland. The train connection between Dublin and Galway is easy enough, but recently when I was invited to read at the Kenny-Naughton Literary Festival in a tiny village called Aghamore in what seemed to me a remote part of County Mayo, I learned that remote is a state of mind.

I am driven from Dublin airport to Aghamore by an Anglo-Irishman named Peter Jackson, a dark-haired talkative man of great patience who teaches high school in the western Danish town of Struer (pop. 10,000) at the base of Limfjord where the oysters are the best I have ever tasted. Peter also invites me to stay a night on his Uncle Jim Coleman's farm in Roscommon, nearby. Then Jim Coleman's 10-year-old granddaughter, Claire, googled me, told her teacher what she had learned from my website and, via Peter Jackson, asked me to bring some of my "stories for children" to share with her school class.

How could I ever say no to a free trip to Ireland or to a 10-year-old girl who lives in a tiny village and is interested enough in literature to google a little-known Irish-American writer who lives in Denmark, excited that I would be visiting, even though I have not written more than a couple of stories which would be suitable "for children"?

Colm O'Donnell, the author, and Peter Jackson at the Aghamore festival

It seems I am to read at the so-called "Kenny/Naughton Autumn School," 28-30 October 2011. My host is the chairman of the event, Paul W. D. Roger, who co-hosts it with the Mayo Arts Office and with Bill Naughton's widow, Ernas—who was born in Austria and resides in the Isle of Man where Bill died in 1992s—as patron. Paul Rogers' e-mails are laconic but he, I am to learn, is anything but laconic; he is the polar opposite of laconic I will learn as he drives me in his brand new black Jaguar sedan around the vast farmlands of elephant grass surrounding Aghamore, on narrow dirt roads, to be shown, inter alia, the tiny cross on the side of one such road where the writer, P. D. Kenny (1862-1944), at the age of 82, fell, suddenly dead, from his bicycle. Kennyy once described himself as "the most unpopular man in Ireland..."

But I am getting ahead of my story.

Peter Jackson drives me from Dublin airport in a rented black Volkswagon to the Claremorris Hotel, just south of Knock, where I am to spend my first night. It is one of the modern buildings thrown up after a local priest successfully lobbied for funds to have the airport at Knock constructed at a cost of somewhere over 70 million Euros. The expense was justified by the fact that enough pilgrims want to flock to the area to see where Our Lady of Knock appeared on the evening of August 21st, 1879 to Mary McLoughlin, the housekeeper of the parish priest; Mary was astonished that evening to see the outside south wall of the church bathed in a mysterious light: There, in short, were apparitions of the Blessed Virgin, St. Joseph, and St. John. In 1971, the Church approved that the apparition was "quite possible"—sufficient recognition to merit an airport at Knock which has increased tourism to the area manyfold.

In the Claremorris Hotel, where Peter Jackson is to collect me early that evening for the opening of the literary festival, a ballroom dancing festival is also about to begin. The lobby is crowded with enthusiastic chesty men in blue blazers and neckties and women in delightfully dressy dresses. I've always been a sucker for a comely adult woman in a comely dress, and the woman who sits down beside me on the lobby sofa, wearing an elegant gray and white silk cocktail dress, sits in fact on my Burberry and is ignoring me in an irresistible manner. But I haven't time to dally. I have to go out into the dark and into the rain. Gently I tug my coat from beneath her—happy that coat! as Bloom might have said—and she turns to me.

"Are you leavin' me, then?" she asks.

"Alas I must but it's breakin' me heart," says I which earns me a reward of the twinkling of her blue eyes and that quality of smile that women on occasion dole out to a man who passes her muster.

We have difficulty finding the restaurant where the evening dinner is to be held, and the rented black 4-door Volkswagon wanders back and forth on the rain-sleeked side roads for some time before we find the place, tucked away in a wood. Only one other person has shown up for the dinner, and the Chair, Paul Rogers, has to hurry off for he has to reprint the program. The reason for this is that the fellow who is one of the main speakers has returned, shaken, to London by train since he is terrified of flying and has been seriously unsettled by the flight into Knock.

So the evening dinner is attended only by myself, Peter, and Mrs. Ginny Waln, a widowed American woman who is bravely and with dignity weathering her macular degeneration. She lived in Cape May, New Jersey, until she and her husband retired here because they had spent happy vacations in Aghamore for many years. Now she is alone, and I offer my arm to lead her to the empty table in the back of the restaurant; a receptionist at the door asks us, "Do you have tickets? You'll need tickets." The woman on my arm says, in New Jersey-accented English, "Pay her no mind. She doesn't know what she's talking about." Ginny, Peter and I dine on salmon and Indian chicken and merlot and then we're off to the festival opening.

The 150+-year-old pub—once also a funeral chapel—that has been closed since 1961 and opens once a year for the Kenny-Naughton Autumn School Literary Festival

By nine p.m. we find the venue, a pub that was founded by one William Waldron in 1862 and inherited by the Rogers' family—Paul's father—in 1956, allowed to function until 1961, when the bartender moved to America, whereupon Paul's father, because he was a teetotaler, he shut it down. It opens only once a year for the Kenny/Naughton Autumn School literary festival. The pub has clearly been closed for fifty years. (No one seems to have noticed that this is the 50th anniversary of its closure.) The bottles on the shelves behind the bar are jacketed in dust. Only a handful of people are present yet, but Paul's brother, T. J. Rogers, young and tall and smilingly taciturn, has set up a Guiness tap behind the bar and draws a glass for me. He explains that the previous publican was not only Aghamore's bar owner but also its mortician. When the Rogers brothers unsealed the pub to ready it for the festival nineteen years ago, two coffins were in evidence on the bar, presumably empty. The other area of the bar is for the living and the thirsty.

T. J. pulls out from beneath the bar a stack of shrouds, some still folded and in their original cellophane wrapping, with an inspection number on them. They are sewn from an odd, shiny material of a brown color with tassels roughly over the nipples and legends inscribed down the breast, some in French, some in Latin, some in English:

Sacred Heart of Jesus, I place my trust in Thee.
Je suis L'immaculée concepcion
Conceptio Immaculata Sum

Those still wrapped are labeled "The Dublin Shroud & Frilling Co., Ltd., 32 Parnell Square, Dublin 1" and have style numbers on them—Habit 901, Habit 566, Habit 364.

"I suppose the customers could not complain about the fit or style," someone comments. T. J. says, "These are at least seventy years old," and produces a cap of the same shiny material and odd brown color that would have been placed on the head of the corpse—it looks rather like a brown dunce's cap. I wonder if the color is meant to symbolize the earth.

The fireplaces are loaded not with peat, but wood, and they crackle, giving heat and light in each of the four rooms of the pub, fighting the chill that emanates off the solid white stone walls. Paul—a bright, smooth-faced man in his mid-forties with black hair, whose shirt is sufficiently unbuttoned to reveal the grey-black curls on his chest—moves about the rooms of the pub, speaking rapid, word-filled greetings to each person by turn. Finally, around ten p.m., he tells me it is almost time to start, and T.J. kindly taps me another Guinness. I am reminded of social events at conferences in Spain and Portugal where drinks and tapas were served until eleven p.m. whereafter the guests were invited to the dinner table. I trust this event will not follow that model.

By now, there are perhaps twenty-five people present with one or two stepping in out of the rain every few minutes. I take a seat next to the stone wall which radiates a flesh-penetrating chill. I gaze longingly at the crackling fireplace across and down-room from me.

At the wobbly blond lectern, Paul Rogers leads off with a few words about Bill Naughton and P.D. Kenny. Bill Naughton (1910-1992) is best known as the author of *Alfie*—both novel and screenplay, which was Michael Caine's breakthrough film in 1966. The screenplay won Naughton an Academy Award nomination that year. He was born in Ballyhaunis, Mayo. Though the Naughton family moved to England in 1914, Aghamore remembers Bill. A plaque commemorating his visit to Aghamore in 1945 is on view at the village square. (I am later to learn that Bill's granddaughter, Anita, who waitressed for ten years at Tea & Sympathy in Greenwich Village in New York, published a book in 2002 about the restaurant.)

Paul's words turn to P. D. Kenny (1862-1944), born in Aghamore, later moving to England where he would become a friend of Winston Churchill, then returning, a writer of social critique with a crisp, lipped

British accent that could only have annoyed the local Republicans. Kenny was requested by Yeats and Lady Gregory to chair a debate about Synge's *The Playboy of the Western World*—which startled him sufficiently to express his surprise because he had thought himself "surely the most unpopular man in all Ireland." Kenny ended his days impecunious enough that he wound up sleeping in his own barn after losing the house he had inherited from his parents. However, a fine headstone has been erected on his grave.

It is these two writers we are gathered in this shut-down pub to celebrate. The celebrants that first night are myself, Hazzel McLynn-Lloyd, and Colm O'Donnell. I am grateful that my reading – from my novel *In the Company of Angels* (Bloomsbury, 2010)—is first; I would not like to have followed either, most especially not O'Donnell.

Colm O'Donnell is a farmer, forester, shepherd and sheep dog trainer from South Sligo, about whom it has been written that his "voice is as sweet and soulful as the tune of his flute." This evening he gives a performance which consists of equal parts song, philosophy, rhythmic step with the heel of his boot on the bare wood floor, the song of his voice and the song of his flute. He concludes his presentation by singing acappella a waltz while spinning Hazel who, when he picked her out to dance with him, whispered anxiously to me, "This was not planned!" Yet she dances beautifully, gracefully plump with an appealing pretty face, just as she gracefully read selections from Naughton's work. Naughton needs, however, no memorial for anyone who is old enough to remember Alfie as Michael Caine (and Dionne Warwick) and not Jude Law.

After the sessions, T. J. is there drafting glasses of stout, and where the coffins might have been, sandwiches and cakes are spread out on the bar. But soon the widow Waln is ready to be taken home, and Peter and I, having traveled since early morning, seize the opportunity to take an early night. I halfway hope that the ballroom dance festival is still in swing at the Claremorris Hotel so that I might see the sparkling-eyed lady who sat on my Burbury, but by the time I get back only the men remain, smoking and swayingly hoisting pints beneath the dripping overhang outside the glass doors, tie knots broken, jackets hanging open.

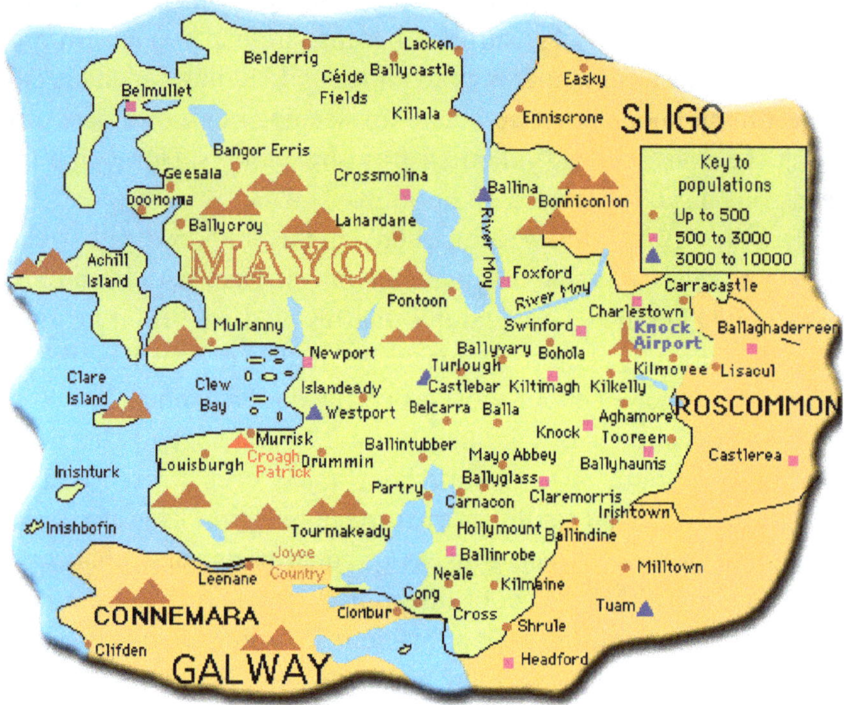

Visitor's map of County Mayo: Here is Cong, location of the Homeric fist fight between Victor McLaglen and John Wayne in the film *The Quiet Man*; Westport, location of Matt Molloy's; Achill Island, location of the Heinrich Böll Cottage; Knock, where it is "quite probable" the Blessed Virgin appeared in 1879; Aghamore, location of the annual Kenny-Naughton festival. To the south is Galway and the Aran Islands where Miss Ivors tries in vain to interest Gabriel Conroy in visiting in Joyce's "The Dead."

In the morning, with great effort, I resist a full Irish breakfast, then am off, feeling virtuous, with Peter and his 84-year-old Uncle Jim to explore the green rolling expanses of grass in the valley of the Partry Mountains.

We stop for a lunch of vegetable soup in the Percy French Hotel in Stokestown, Co. Roscommon. French (1854-1920) wrote many songs that my father used to sing in New York—"Abdul Abulbul Amir," "The Mountains of Mourne," "Eileen Oge (The Pride of Petravail)," about how the hardest-featured man in Petravail stole away the prettiest girl in town by ignorning her

Boys, oh, boys, with fate it's hard to grapple
Of me eye, boys, Eileen was the apple
And now to see her walkin' to the chapel
With the hardest-featured man in Petravail
Boys oh boys, hear me when I say
When you do your courtin' make no mistake
If ye want them to run after you
Then look the other way
Cause they're mostly like the Pride of Petravail.

French was born near Elphin in Roscommon and is commemorated by at least two bronze figures of himself on public benches—in the main square of Ballyjamesduff (one of his songs is "Come Back Paddy Reilly to Ballyjamesduff"—which means "The Town of Black James" in Anglicized Irish) as well as a bench on the Grand Canal in south Dublin, just across from the bench on which sits a likeness of Patrick Kavanagh (1905-67), author of the masterful "The Great Hunger" (which is not about the potato famine).

We decide to visit Achill Island to see the Heinrich Böll Cottage—a writers colony. On the way we stop in Westport, a town of perhaps twenty thousand, where we take a pint at Matt Molloy's on the high street. Jimmy the bartender, it turns out, is a son of Matt Molloy, the flutist of the Chieftains who played the haunting theme song, "Women of Ireland," from Stanley Kubrick's 1975 film version of Thackeray's 1844 novel *Barry Lyndon*. I ask Jimmy if he is a musician, and he tells me he is more interested in surfing, will be visiting Australia soon to do so.

Back in the car, up and down hills, weaving through corkscrew squiggles of the narrow roads, the black VW rolls north along the N59 toward Achill—the largest Irish island. Henrich Böll, born in Cologne in 1917, had visited Achill regularly during the 1950s and '60s; his experiences of western Ireland are described in his book Irish Journal. Böll won the Nobel Prize for Literature in 1972 and died in 1985.

Our literature about Achill describes that the quality of the light has attracted many artists to spend time there—Alexander Williams, Robert Henri, and Marie Howet.

However, the light on this overcast late October day, as we roll across the causeway onto the island, is less than inspiring. The fields and hills stretch and roll desolately, gray-white sheep grazing here and there in the charcoal gray grass.

We stop at the Achill Sound Hotel to ask directions to the Böll Cottage, and the man we ask—perhaps starved for an audience—couches the directions he gives in a nonstop monologue which flows so quickly I cannot follow its connections and am soon lost among his well-intentioned words. I notice once again that the Irish are forever telling jokes but seldom laughing.

Following what we think are his directions, we are soon on what seems to be the wrong road. Uncle Jim, from the back seat, looks out over the flowing, sloping gray meadows and says, "You wouldn't want to spend the winter here."

Peter hails down a large van at a crossing. The woman driving says she will lead us to the cottage and takes off speeding through the curving hills so that we keep losing sight of her. Finally, however, she stops and points to a low series of buildings which apparently is the Cottage. She does a broken-U and is gone as the two of us step out of the VW into the damp wind—Uncle Jim opts to remain in the warm, dry automobile.

A sign on the gate identifies Böll Cottage. In German and English, it requests respect for the privacy of the artists in residence. It is clear to me that were I to spend any length of time here, privacy would be the last thing I desired – but I am a city boy who feels hemmed in by open space, no longer at home in a town that has fewer than Copenhagen's 1,525 serving houses.

The program for the second night of the festival includes a reading by myself from my newest novel (*Falling Sideways*, Bloomsbury, 2011), a reading of poetry by Iggy McGovern, a professor of physics at Trinity College in Dublin who has published two collections of poems, and a story by Tom Heneghan who, the program tells, was born in Belcarra "in the year of the big snow." There is also a storyteller, Vincent Pearse, who tells one about a woman who roasts a drake and, because her guests do not show up, eats the whole bird by herself, then goes to the priest to confess the sin of gluttony, but she cannot remember the word so she attempts instead to describe the irresistibility of her temptation: "Ah there he was, Father, lyin' there on the table with his beautiful brown skin and his lovely brown legs spread open. I couldn't help but devour him, Father. Then I was hungry for him again in the morning and had a bit more of him then, too, Father. What was left of him, I fed to the dogs." Vincent Pearse's talents are clearly Homeric for he is still by the fire place, still surrounded by a group of enraptured people when Peter and I slip away at half past midnight.

In the morning, after a comfortable night's sleep on Uncle Jim's farm, we briefly meet young Claire, whose shyness my very best smile and banter fail to unlock—though I will discover after we have left in the VW that she has slipped a note in my bag:

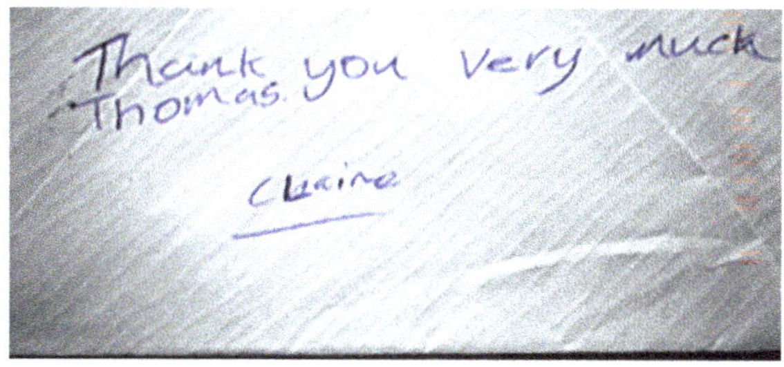
Thank you very much Thomas.

Claire

Peter and I stop by the Aghamore home of Paul Rogers who, after tea, races us about the tiny unpaved roads in his new black Jaguar to show us Bill Naughton's mother's place, P. D. Kenny's farm, the cross on the side of a dirt road where P. D. Kenny expired while cycling, a place where a school house used to be that Kenny attended. All amidst the fields of elephant grass which feed the sheep and cow

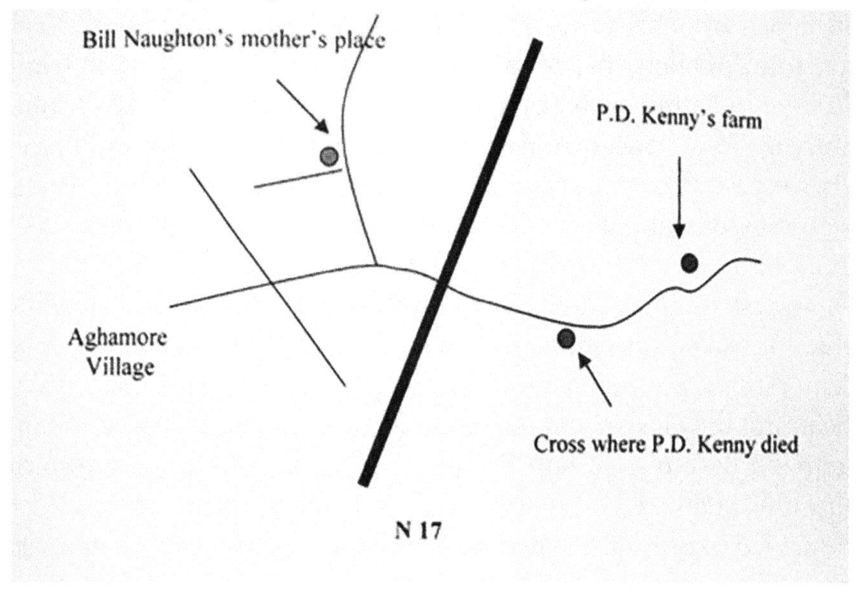

A primitive map of Aghamore

It seems a lonely place, and I recall Peter's Uncle Jim saying the day before, "You wouldn't want to spend a winter there." But perhaps I have developed a fear of nature, a fear of open emptiness, a fear of silence. Which makes me think of Sean O'Faolain's remarkable story about the death of the last great story-teller, "The Silence of the Valley."

As we pull in outside Paul's house again, to pick up Peter's rented car, there is a collie racing around the Jaguar. I ask if that is Paul's dog, and he says, "Ah, no. That dog is quite mad," and I realize that the collie is trying to herd the Jag to the point that I fear it will be crushed beneath the wheels, but the dog is too quick and intent on getting the car to do as it ought.

Time is short to make our flight from Dublin, and we still have to cross a wide stretch of the country, but I have already decided that there is no sense in worrying: I have surrendered myself to the meandering roads and hairpin turns of Irish time. And sure enough Peter's rented VW is delivered back to the airport in Dublin with nearly a half hour to spare before our flight.

As we are herded through security, removing belts, shoes, jackets, emptying pockets, I notice a familiar tune playing on the Muzak which it takes me a moment to place: It is the theme from *Alfie*. It occurs to me that I will never have the same relation to that song, will never hear it without thinking of the elephant grass, the dusty pub, the music, the shrouds, the stories, the stout, the people—Paul, T.J., Peter, Uncle Jim, Claire, Ginny, Colm O'Donnell, Hazel, Breda, all of them—and of those days of cordiality in Aghamore.

DEATH, SEX, AND SIN IN FAIRYTALE BRUGES/BRUGGE

Walter Cummins

"Bruges is a shithole." So says Raymond (Colin Farrell) at the beginning of Martin McDonagh's ingenious 2008 film, *In Bruges*. Raymond and his hit man partner, Ken (Brendan Gleeson), after bungling a killing in London have been dispatched by their gangster boss, Harry (Ralph Fiennes), to that Flemish city, ostensibly to lay low for a short time. In his first hours after checking into a hotel overlooking a canal, Ray finds the notion of two weeks in Bruges a torture of boredom. A scene later, the two of them in a canal boat exploring the magnificent medieval architecture of the city, Ray sulks, disgusted at just "looking at stuff." The more aesthetic Ken tells him it's called "sight-seeing."

Though Ray's denial serves as an ironic joke for those who know the city as a magnet of contemporary tourism or are just watching the stunning scenery on the screen, his attitude mirrors that of the protagonists in Georges Rodenbach's late nineteenth-century novels and stories set in Bruges. They wander the streets along the canals on foot and see nothing but a morbid bleakness. In several senses McDonagh picks up where Rodenbach left off, even though the contexts are opposite, Rodenbach's setting a bleak place forgotten by history, McDonagh's a rare European treasure.

In the film it turns out coldblooded Harry cherishes a youthful memory of Bruges as a "fairytale" city and wants to give Ray a final pleasure before ordering Ken to shoot him for accidentally killing a small boy in a London church with one of the bullets meant for the real target, a priest. In Bruges, churches are very prominent, turning out to be significant in the film just as they are in Rodenbach's fiction.

Without spoiling more for those who have not yet seen the movie, at the end, a bullet-riddled Ray being rushed down a hospital corridor on a gurney, says in a voice-over, "... maybe that's what hell is: the entire rest of eternity spent in fuckin' Bruges." Yet he decides he really doesn't want to die.

Of course, despite Harry's murderous relationship with reality, the vast majority of those who visit Bruges today would agree with his fairytale assessment. Ray is unique in finding it a shithole. Large open squares, majestic churches, winding canals, cobblestone streets, masterpieces of Flemish art, green parks along the water, one fine chocolate shop after another, endless varieties of beers, heaping plates of steamed mussels. If that's hell, it's hard to imagine how heaven could improve.

Note that you won't find the name Bruges anywhere on the streets. For the locals, as it is on the maps and T-shirts and souvenir mugs, it's Brugge (pronounced Brew-hah by the natives). That's the Flemish name for a city in Flanders, and the Flemish harbor rivalry, if not enmity, towards the French-speaking Walloons in the east of Belgium. The tension is both cultural and political, prosperous Flanders seeking greater in independence, claiming that it funds the economically laggard Walloons.

When we visited Brugge in October 2013, after the high season, the Markt (the Market Square) and surrounding area still teemed with tourists chattering in multiple tongues, spilling off the narrow sidewalks onto the cobblestone streets, blocking cars and the steady stream of horse-drawn carriages. These visitors packed the canal boats, shops, restaurants, churches, and museums, clustering under umbrellas when it rained, all eager to see and discover. We didn't notice a Ray among them. After all, Bruges/Brugge is a UN World Heritage Site, as it certainly deserves to be.

But it wasn't always so, certainly not in Rodenbach's vision. Over a number of centuries Brugge went from being one of Europe's major cities to centuries as a moribund backwater and now to a flourishing destination of global tourism, drawing three to four million visitors a year. Harry notes to Ken what most tourists know: it's a perfectly preserved medieval city. Harry also contends that if it weren't in Belgium, it would draw many more, though fitting them in would be a huge, perhaps insurmountable, problem.

Brugge began as Bryghia ("landing stage") in the ninth century when the Normans invaded its then harbor with plundering ships. It soon flourished into one of northern Europe's major shipping and commercial centers, its fourteenth century population of 35,000 then as large as London's. Brugge reached its peak in the fifteenth century when Italian bankers, including the Medici, set up branches and the Dukes of Burgundy chose the city for their main residence. The great artists of the Flemish School of Primitive Painting, such as Jan van Eyck and Hans Melming, were drawn by the wealth. Brugge became the largest cultural capital north of the Alps.

The glory was short-lived because by the end of its glory century the city lost access to the sea when the harbor silted up and merchants relocated a bit north to the shipping center of Antwerp, which still offers one of Europe's best deep-water ports. The Dukes moved away, and the economy declined, the population surviving at the edges of poverty for the next four hundred years. That misfortune suffered by all those generations turned out to be a benefit to today's visitors. Without capital, the city lacked the ability to change and develop, so no new building took place and, as a result, nothing was torn down. Thus, the purity of preservation.

A rebirth began in the early nineteenth century when English soldiers who had defeated Napoleon at Waterloo began to bring their families to see the battleground and soon decided to emigrate because their pensions would go so much further in Brugge. The English appreciated the art and architecture, its large colony remaining until the outbreak of World War One. The city was spared bombing and occupation during both twentieth century world wars, coming close to destruction in the second when German Commander Immo Hopman was ordered to literally bring the city to ruin. But he refused to obey, calling the order madness because "Bruges is the most beautiful town for miles around."

At the end of the nineteenth century, in addition to being lured by enthusiastic English guidebooks, thousands of tourists were drawn to the city to see the setting of Rodenbach's best-selling 1892 symbolist short novel, *Bruges-la-Morte* (*Dead Bruges*). Huysmans and Mallarme praised it as a high point in decadent writing. Rodenbach, in this novel, as in other works, depicts Bruges as a gloomy, empty, religion-dominated, and haunted environment, his isolated protagonists torn by guilt and failure, lust and passion their downfall.

Ironically—although most of the film *In Bruges* displays noisy, populated streets and squares, while Rodenbach's are bleak and empty, but for a few Beguine nuns and an occasional religious procession—the movie and the fiction have much in common. In many of the film's final chase scenes those streets become empty and menacing. Sex, violence, sin, spiritual guilt and contrition dominate in both works, even though the film is very funny black humor and the novel darkly glum. Several of Rodenbach's characters do end up experiencing a hellish version of "the entire rest of eternity spent in fuckin' Bruges." Without the expletive, of course.

In his brief foreword to *Bruges-la-Morte*, Rodenbach explains that he considers the urban landscapes "fundamentally involved in the plot of the novel." (The translation of the work by Philip Mosely won France's 2008 Prix de la Traduction Littéraire.) Rodenbach goes on to list the centrality of "quays, deserted streets, old residences, canals, Beguinage, churches, belfries, cult objects" and the tall towers whose shadows lengthen over the text.

His protagonist, Hughes Viane, possesses enough wealth to spend all his days in a first floor bedroom, idly reading, smoking, and immersing in memories of his youngdead wife, just thirty at her demise. He then goes for late afternoon walks along the quays, having chosen Bruges after she died because of his desire for a "dead city" to correspond to his dead wife:

> As he wandered about on this particular evening, black memories haunted him more than ever, merging from beneath bridges where faces cry from invisible sources. A sensation of death emanated from the shuttered houses, from windows like eyes blurred in the throes of death, from gables tracing crape stairways in the water. [...] And everywhere he went, the small salty notes of the parish bells dropped on his head, as if flung from a brush during an absolution.

The first chapter reveals that Viane cut off a spray of his dead wife's braided hair to memorialize in a crystal case he could gaze at every day. Like a Chekhov gun, that braid will figure at the very end of the story when Jane, a crude, sensual dancer, the wife's look-alike whom Viane maintains in a separate residence to satisfy his lust, finally to Viane's shame enters his house while a cortege of worshippers passes on the street outside, carrying the sacred vessel supposedly containing Christ's blood from the Basilica of the Holy Blood. At the peak of Viane's tormented struggle between sex and guilt, Jane, furious at being dumped, smashes the crystal preserving the wife's hair (note the parallel with the vessel of the Holy Blood), and in an even greater, irrational fury Viane strangles Jane with that rope of hair.

While this frenzy takes place between two people alone in a private room, the violent shootings at the end of *In Bruges* occur on a snowy night in a public square at Christmas time in the midst of a scene being filmed for a movie, many of the milling performers in surreal costumes, reminiscent of figures in Hieronymus Bosch's hell. Still, the two works embody themes of guilt and expiation.

While Rodenbach's fiction exudes somberness, and the movie evokes a complex mix of comic irony and a genuine need for expiation, the two share the angst of atoning for misdeeds.

Worship versus lust provides the tension of another Rodenbach short novel, *Hans Cadzand's Vocation.* The title character, overwhelmed by his religious education, seeks to dedicate himself to God and join an order in nearby Ghent. But his long-widowed mother's greatest fear is loss of the company of her handsome son. She wants him married and living nearby. But, after he rejects the love of the appealing Wilhelmine, Mevr. Cadzand hires a pretty housemaid Ursula, who "had such an innocent air, all the better to seduce him." And seduce him she does, luring him into long sessions of passion that Hans' mother believes will give him a taste for life, "now that he knows the rose in full bloom, the secret rose of the flesh!" Instead his guilt for this sexual sin destroys Hans' vocation. He feels himself too impure and contaminated. Ursula is dismissed, and Mevr. Cadzand ends up with her son at home; but he is a shell of a man, "ardent in prayer," attending daily mass. Yet, "It was beyond remedy. God no longer wanted him, no longer sought him."

Sex is hardly as grim in *In Bruges*, despite the scene of Ray, Ken, and an American dwarf, Jimmy, whose size is key to the film's crucial ironic misunderstanding, in a room with two prostitutes snorting coke. The women are stoned, the dwarf launches into a racist tirade, and Ken leaves in disgust. No sex happens. Nor does the relationship of Ray and Chloe, a pretty Dutch drug dealer who had been involved with a petty skinhead thief, find consummation. But they do fall in love, spending much of the film's final minutes, before Harry arrives with a revolver, exchanging one kiss after another at a table in the Markt.

Unlike sex in Rodenbach, the film's transgression is murder, especially that of a child. Ray's original blunder on his first hit assignment took place in a church, where the priest in the confessional box was his intended target and the child unintended collateral damage. In a scene that takes place in the Basilica of the Holy Blood near the City Hall in Brugge's Burg Square, Ken stands at the altar to lament his transgressions as an assassin, Ray not quite getting it at this point.

Later the two of them stare at Hieronymus Bosch's "Last Judgment" in the city's major art museum, viewing the torments of the damned alluded to at the film's climax. The more astute Ken understands its

message for him, and eventually, Ray, seated by the statue of Jan van Eyck, breaks down in tears over the killing of the child, soon becoming suicidal.

The film, brimming with very clever dialogue and comic ironies, creates a dilemma: what to do with likable characters guilty of killing for money. Harry, the man who has ordered the hits, is hardly as appealing. But he too ends up in Bruges. Hans Cadzand's obsessive prayer is not the answer for these three. Hughes Viane's in murdering his temptress with a braid of hair comes closer. The movie's deaths spatter blood in the Markt, as do the multiple gunshots that riddle Ray.

Relating Rodenbach's fictions of Bruges to a film about that city more than a century later may appear to justify the author's association of Bruges with death and Ray's speculation that it's a shithole form of hell. But for those of us who join the millions of tourist visitors, Bruges is Harry's fairyland. We glide down its canals, marvel at its architecture, wonder at its art, drink its many beers, devour its abundance of gourmet chocolates. Some of those venturing into its churches kneel and light candles, but the great majority snap photos or pan videos, awed by the art of stained glass, sculptures, and paintings. All that passion is history, a subject for creative genius. Everyone should see Brugge. Even Ray wants to survive for Chloe, even if it means living there.

A VISIT TO *HUNGER* 120 YEARS LATER

Thomas E. Kennedy

> "It was in those days when I wandered about hungry in Kristiania, that strange city which no one leaves before It has set its mark upon him..."
>
> —Knut Hamsun, Hunger

My introduction to Knut Hamsun's novel *Hunger* was via Henning Carlsen's 1966 film with Per Oscarsson's magical portrayal of the main character. The film led me to read an SAS Airline bilingual publication (Scandinavian Words 15) of the first chapter, written by Hamsun in the late 1880s and later expanded to the novel. The novel was set in Kristiania (Oslo) in 1890—120 years ago—and the main character, a starving author, is writing a piece entitled Crimes of the Future.

Hunger is a journey, a visit to a place, a "strange city which no one leaves before it has set its mark upon him..." It is about being there, descending into it, if you will, and about leaving again in time to evade complete dissolution in madness and living to tell the tale. To some extent, the book is autobiographical, and one can trace the forward trajectory of its fictional main character via the real person of Hamsun and where he goes when he leaves Kristiania (the former name of Oslo, the Norwegian capital, when it was under the Danes and then the Swedes) and what happens to him then.

In fact, in the late summer of 1888, Hamsun sailed home from the United States to Copenhagen and stopped in the Norwegian capital only because the ship docked there for twenty-four hours. Previously, earlier in the 1880s, Hamsun experienced hunger, cold and poverty not only in Oslo, but also in Chicago in the winter of 1886-7, all of which informs his powerful novel.

But what happened to him standing at the rail of that ship (Jan Kjæstad tells us, in his introduction to the SAS version of the early fragment of the book) looking out at the city of Oslo from the deck, is that an enlightened sentence occurred to him, and much like the main character of Hunger, he scribbled it down—the sentence which later became so famous that virtually any reasonably educated citizen of Norway, and many elsewhere, can utter it by heart: "It was in those days that I wandered about hungry in Kristiania, that strange city which no one leaves before it has set its mark upon him..."

Hamsun then proceeded on that boat to Copenhagen, wrote the

first fragment of what would become a full-length novel, showed it to the editor of one of Denmark's leading newspapers, Edvard Brandes, brother of the prominent literary critic, Georg Brandes, and Brandes told him, "You can look forward to a very great future." Brandes had recognized what readers of the fragment would also see when it appeared anonymously in the literary journal *Ny Jord* (New Earth), that Hamsun had revolutionized Scandinavian literature, perhaps in some ways world literature, considering the effect his writing had on writers as diverse as Thomas Mann, Ernest Hemingway, Franz Kafka and Andre Gide. In an essay entitled, "From the Unconscious Life of the Mind," Hamsun himself described the book that was to follow from that fragment as "a book about the delicate fluctuations of a sensitive soul, the strange, peculiar life of the mind, the mysteries in the nerves of a starving body."

The novel is the story of a journey at the heart of *Hunger* as surely as the journey at the heart of Conrad's darkness. The journey begins with the unnamed main character already in Kristiania (Oslo) and it ends when he leaves "that strange city which no one leaves before it has set its mark upon him." The journey is into hunger, a visit into the strange city of hunger, but it is no mere hungering for food; it is a hunger to seek what is true and real without compromise and to preserve one's dignity and autonomy, which in fact intoxicates and leads one to the edge of madness and which is conflicted always by the fact that the hunger of the body leads to compromise—a willingness to work at meaningless jobs instead of seeking what might be real and true beyond that hunger. And one can exist in such a place for only so long before being driven into madness and despair.

Anyone who has not read Hamsun's powerful novel or even the first fragment which gave birth to the novel or seen the Henning Carlsen film from 1966—with its magical performance by Per Oscarsson (I don't believe I have ever seen a performance on film that matches his achievement in that one) is urged to do so.

You have a great experience in store.

A tragic and macabre footnote to this tale of a visit to a book inspired by the capital city of Norway: Per Oscarsson, the Swedish actor who played the starving character in that film and also played in the film versions of the very popular Stieg Larsson books, on December 30th, 2010, at the age of 83, burned to death with his younger wife in their isolated home in the Swedish countryside. The wind was so violent that night that it blew away the smoke which might otherwise have awakened Oscarsson and his wife. The house burnt so completely that nothing was left standing but the chimney, and the authorities had to sift through the ash for days before finding remains of the Oscarssons amongst it. But Per Oscarsson's performance in *Hunger* made him as near to immortal as one can come.

This essay first appeared, in altered form, in *Absinthe: New European Literature,* issue 14, 2010.

A LOCATION FOR HIRE
Broughton Castle

Walter Cummins

FOR ANYONE WHO TAKES WHAT THEY SEE in a movie literally, Broughton Castle, as depicted in *Shakespeare in Love,* exists on the banks of the Thames, just a short boat trip from London. Thanks to the miracle of filmmaking, this setting comes across as geographically accurate, when in fact Broughton Castle is located miles from London, deep in the Oxfordshire countryside in the midst of an open field and surrounded by a moat.

I knew that when I saw the movie. What I was wrong about wasn't geography but rather the reason the castle was allowed to be used as a setting for certain scenes. I had assumed a family favor. Joseph Fiennes, the actor who played the young Shakespeare and brother of Ralph, is also a cousin of the Fiennes family that provides the Lords Saye and Sele, the barons who are the castle's owners and inhabitants (full name Twisleton-Wykeham-Fiennes). Why not help a relative further his career, I thought. Instead, as I learned from a 2009 memoir, *The Music Room* by William Fiennes, a younger son of the current Lord Saye and Sele, being an aristocrat doesn't pay the accumulating bills for maintaining a medieval manor house and gardens. To garner income, the property has to be rented out for events, including filming of movies and TV shows. Scenes from the 1994 *Madness of King George* are set there, as well as from the TV production of *Wolf Hall*, other movies, TV shows, commercials, concerts, and fashion shot settings.

In *Shakespeare in Love*, the castle serves as the de Lesseps home of young Will's love, Viola (Gwyneth Paltrow). Will first meets Viola in the Great Hall. Later, in the Oak Room, Lord Wessex (Colin Firth) informs Viola of her planned marriage, a threat that adds a Shakespearean tension to the love story. While a studio set was used for her bedroom, for the exterior, a false wooden Juliet-like balcony was built onto the castle to overlook the formal gardens.

Capturing his boyhood memories, Joseph Fiennes calls the arrival of performers and production crews "invasions," the crews arriving like "desert caravans, grey production trucks inching through the gatehouse, the car park a camp of Winnebagos." A child of five or so, he wandered the set-crammed and brightly lit rooms of his home, meeting the likes of Ian McKellen, Jane Seymour, and Richard Chamberlain dressed as Prince Charming. He tells of his parents' constant worry over damage to the historic furnishing, his father haunting the sets, "vigilant for carelessness."

Today the castle's website touts "Location Hire":

> It is an ideal film location being only just over one hours' drive from West London. Exteriors and interiors provide a range of different location opportunities—unspoilt parkland, gatehouse, moat, battlements, fortified manor house / castle, chapel, great hall, picture gallery, library, dining room, armour, and wonderful gardens including the formal Ladies' Garden. A range of styles are apparent —mediaeval, Tudor / Elizabethan, and some gothic interiors.

The original manor house was built about 1300 by Sir John de Broughton, who sold it to William of Wykeham, Bishop of Winchester and Chancellor of England, bought the house in 1377. Around seventy years later the property passed to the Fiennes family when in 1448 William's great-nephew Sir Thomas Wykeham's granddaughter, Margaret married Sir William Fiennes, later the second Lord Saye and Sele.

The property endured literal ups and downs, major renovation and addition of additional stories carried out in the second half of the sixteenth century, only to suffer major damage when captured by the Royalists in the next century's civil war. Over the next several hundred years the Lords Saye and Sele alternated between rebuilding the home and wasting their fortunes, to the point when the seventeenth Lord let the castle in 1886 to the Gordon-Lennox family. Possession returned to the Fiennes family in 1912, with major twentieth-century restoration projects supported by the UK's Historic Buildings Council and English Heritage.

I met the current and twenty-first baron, Nathaniel Fiennes—aged 99 as of this writing—and his wife on a frigid January day in 2003, the couple, small people, walking their corgis on an expanse of frost-covered lawn far from the manor house, which is open to public visitors only in summer. When I say I, I don't mean one-to-one because I was part of a group of writers and MFA students who had walked the three miles from Wroxton Abbey on a free afternoon of a writers' residency. The Lord and his Lady were quite friendly and chatty, bundled against the cold in Barbour jackets and scarves, curious about who our group might be, people with American accents out in the middle of the countryside, far from the typical London and Oxford tourist lures.

We were all gathered near what seemed a large frozen pond but turned out to be just inches of ice formed on a massive puddle when the temperatures plunged after weeks of deluging rain. Standing out in the middle of that faux pond were the future Lord Saye and Sele—Hon. Martin Guy Fiennes—with his wife—the former Kang Chai Lian—and their very young children. He was in conversation with my colleague the novelist David Grand, whose twin sons were at the time the same age as those on the ice. Beyond that coincidence, they shared a rarer one; David and the future Baron, then working at some profession in a London office, knew the same person in New York. What are the odds two people meeting for the first time on a frozen expanse in the English countryside would share an acquaintance three thousand miles away?

In yet another coincidence, another member of our group, the poet-story writer-novelist Terese Svoboda had the evening before picked at random from the Wroxon library William Fiennes' first book, *The Snow Geese*, winner of the Somerset Maugham Award and Hawthornden Prize. She was carrying it with her during our walk, unaware that the day after choosing the book she would see the author's older brother and his birthplace.

Conversations over, most of us shivering as we stood there, we turned left and crossed the small bridge and passed through the gate to parish church of St Mary the Virgin and then, after navigating the graveyard, a couple hundred yards farther for an excellent meal at the upscale Saye and Sele Arms pub, one with linen tablecloths, decorated with tankards hanging from the ceiling beams.

That was the first of several January walks from Wroxton to the grounds of Broughton Castle and libations at the Saye and Sele Arms. In good weather you can get there via footpaths, but during winter the paths are thick with mud. We needed pavement. The route we took was out the gate of Wroxton Abbey, through Wroxton village to the Banbury road, turn left at the historic marker on the single-track road to the village of North Newington, mainly a row of small dwellings on both sides of a long main street, and once past that village turn right after a hillside full of sheep onto path through a growth of trees, then right again to the grounds around the castle.

Tom Kennedy and I made the trek a number of times, on some occasions just the two of us, on others part of a group. When unaccompanied, we reported, hoping to create a myth, that we jogged all the way back and forth to the castle, later adding the embellishment that we tossed large rocks between us as we ran. No one believed us.

One time we were at Broughton with the writer and teacher David Berner on a very foggy day. The castle had a certain mysterious charm when seen in the haze. After yet another fine pub meal the three of us walked briefly along a paved road and then on a path to the town of Banbury, emerging on a main street, past the famous Banbury Cross—destination of a cock horse according to the rhyme, ending up in another pub before taking a taxi back to Wroxton.

My last few Januaries at Wroxton I didn't make the walk to Broughton Castle but did suggest it to others, all returning with reports of a happy day. My visits were vicarious.

I've never seen the inside of the castle, never enjoying the summer open hours. What I imagine about the interior comes from movies and television, and all that is probably a staged deception. Still, I know the moat and the grounds and the exterior, the church and its gravestones, as well as the décor of the local pub. That satisfies.

Photographs are from various Internet sites.

DOSTOEVSKI ON SKINNER STREET
The Booktrader, Skindergade 23, Copenhagen

Thomas E. Kennedy

In a subterranean bookshop on Copenhagen's Skindergade, a man standing behind the counter looks as much like Fyodor Dostoevski as any man I have ever seen. His name is Lars Rasmussen, a fifty-year-old Dane.

Lars Rasmussen, owner and proprietor of The Booktrader, at front desk

Above his head is a long shelf of books which he spent years collecting. They stand on their lower edges, cover out, and their one-letter titles spell out the alphabet, starting with A by Andy Warhol and running 29 volumes, all the way to the last three letters of the Danish alphabet – Æ, Ø, Å (Ø is the Danish word for "island" and is thus the Danish title of that visionary book by Aldous Huxley from 1962, the year before he died on the day JFK was assassinated.).

Lars Rasmussen's alphabet collection of books: "Have you read his F? Oh, yes, but I prefer Q." (James Joyce, *Ulysses*)

Clearly a man who not only sells books, but reads—and writes, edits and publishes—them as well, he explains his wish to assemble this collection of mono-letter titled volumes with a quote from Joyce's Ulysses: "Books you were going to write with letters for titles. Have you read his F? Oh, yes, but I prefer Q. Yes, but W is wonderful. Oh, yes, W." A customer has also contacted Lars to show him the dictionary he has compiled of one-letter words in many languages—he has collected over a thousand of them. And Lars's Booktrader Publishing has, inter alia, published a dictionary for animals—from which a "gris," for example (Danish for "pig"), can look up how to say "oink" in twenty-five different languages.

On the other side of Lars, affixed to the ceiling, is an erotic wreath molded in plaster. It depicts a curling strand of figures engaged in various sexual couplings and wafting like a string of pearls out of a molded book at its center. You wouldn't notice it unless you stood directly beneath it and tipped your head back all the way to study the ceiling above you. Lars engaged the artist, Kasper Holten, to sculpt it for him in 1999.

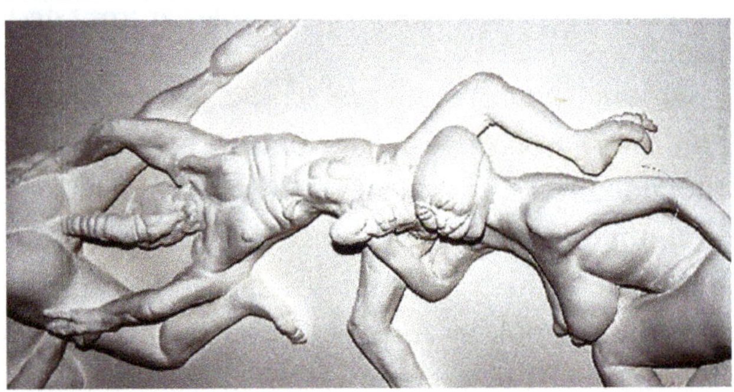

Detail from erotic plaster sculpture from 1999 on ceiling of the Booktrader. Artist: Kasper Holten

In the broad display windows outside the shop are, inter alia, the remains of an eighty-book collection of Joyceana—down to fifty-seven at this writing—and many another thing, including a gathering of sexy-covered noir paperbacks and the CD poetry reading series Lars published on the Booktrader label—an audio documentation of outstanding turn-of-the-century Danish poets—and jazz CDs. Every year he travels to the Cape Town townships with his wife to hear jazz, and his expertise on South African jazz is documented in several volumes on the topic, published by Booktrader Publishing and also displayed in the long front window.

Display of Booktrader CDs of contemporary Danish poets

Behind and around him in the half-basement shop are shelves and tables and shelves and shelves and shelves of books—approximately fifty thousand of them in stock, including the lonely man's table, heaped with used *Playboys* and *Penthouses* on sale for $2.50 apiece. All ripe for a honeymoon of the hand.

Lars Rasmussen has owned the Booktrader since 1988. The shop originally opened five years prior to that, in 1983, by its founder, the American David Grubb and his Norwegian-Danish partner, Bodil Bødker-Næss. I know Lars hardly at all, but am on my way this mild May day of Copenhagen demonstrations against government cuts in welfare to spend an afternoon interviewing and getting to know him.

David Grubb I knew well for a time, and Bodil, too. I met them around 1981. Sick of the relentless rejection to which my fiction had been subjected for too many years, I had decided to quit writing—and to quit reading, too. If I couldn't write, I wouldn't read. If no one wanted my stuff, I didn't want theirs either. Living in Copenhagen, I saw an ad in one of the Danish newspapers placed by someone interested in buying second-hand English-language books, of which I had hundreds. The ad had been placed by David Grubb. He came over to our house and selected about 400 books from my shelves, all fiction—I had it in for fiction, didn't want to sell my poetry. I figured he would give me like a dime apiece, but he offered a dollar. He wanted the books to stock an English-language bookshop he was opening. I didn't think he would do very well as a businessman, paying that much for used paperbacks. He was from Indiana, as near as I could figure a kind of hip Quaker businessman booklover, a tall bearded man in his early thirties, maybe five years younger than I. We invited him to stay for dinner, and he called Bodil to come join us, and we spent a pleasant evening together.

Front of The Booktrader on Skindergade with griffin handrails at stairway down to entrance

Two years passed during which time I decided to write one more story, and I knew, I could feel, as it poured out of my pen, that this was my breakthrough. The story, titled "The Sins of Generals," was accepted by *Confrontation* magazine in January 1982. I was so startled by the acceptance that I very nearly withdrew the story, under the Groucho Marx principle that any magazine that wanted a story by me was not a magazine I wanted to be in. But I refrained and instead took Beckett's advice: I went on.

Then I received an invitation from David Grubb to the opening of his bookshop, a wide-faced basement shop, three steps down on Skindergade in the center of Copenhagen. Half the shop was a bookstore, the other half a weavery run by Bodil. The shop was handsomely appointed, and I wandered around, wine glass in hand, examining the titles on the shelves. Every fifth book or so had once been mine, and the penciled prices inside the covers showed that David knew more about business than I had imagined. The books he'd bought from me were priced at ten times or more what I got for them. I'd had no idea how scarce literary books in English were in Denmark. Now that I was a published writer, I was ready to begin reading again and to admit volumes of fiction into my home, so I began to buy them back—at a fat mark up!

No matter, it was a good cause. I liked David, and I liked Bodil, and I liked the shop and the weavery, too, and bought a piece of Bodil's textile art depicting a New York street in night blue with silver light, now hanging on the wall of my son's northside apartment. The shop was roomy and bright and there was a conversation pit at the center of it and interesting customers. A literary gathering place had been born.

Soon David brought in William Burroughs, to have him interviewed in his shop by the legendary Danish poet and performer, Dan Turèll, and the younger poet, Sam Fleischer, and people recognized that David was a serious cultural force. That was the only time I ever saw Burroughs. I'd been expecting a wildman, but was startled to find he was a tall, slim, elegant fellow, wearing a sweater vest under his narrow sports jacket, tie knotted to the throat of his button-down collars, his voice crisp and Brahmin clear.

Poster of William Burroughs appearance in the Booktrader in November 1984. Behind and to Burroughs' right is Knud Odde, bass player for the Danish rock group Sort Sol(Black Sun). To Odde's right is the singer. Rasmussen has an extensive collection of never-before shown photos of Burroughs that he will be putting up for sale when he has finished preparing his Burroughs catalogue

There was a public signing and interview in the shop to launch Burroughs's *Cities of the Red Night,* followed by a stage appearance at the theater Saltlageret (a former salt warehouse) in which Burroughs read from his work. The film from the interview and reading will be incorporated in a Burroughs retrospective documentary currently under production by Lars Movin. Questions for the interview were also devised by Greg Stephenson, an American expatriate writer in Copenhagen who, with his wife Birgit, herself an expert on Paul Bowles, had been editing the English-language magazine *Pearl*—a stapled journal of powerful content and with strong, original art on the cover. During the 1990s—at which time publication of *Pearl* had been taken on by Lars Rasmussen, it was named by the *Library Journal* as one of the ten best literary magazines in the world. Pearl discontinued publication in the late 90s. The two issues I have in my possession—one from 1982, prior to its Booktrader publication period, one from 1993—give a fair idea of the quality of content: George Starbuck, John Ciardi, Ferlinghetti, Neal Cassady, Philip O'Connor, Alan Sillitoe, with covers and illustrations by the distinguished Polish-Danish artist, Teodor Bok.

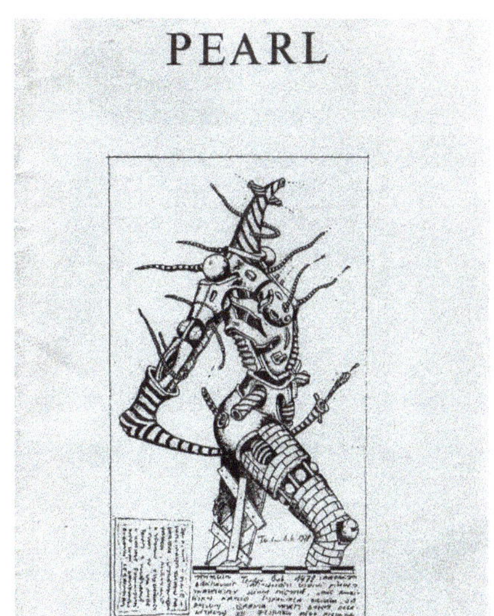

Cover of *Pearl* No. 9, Spring 1982. and Cover of *Pearl* 14, Winter 1993. Cover art of both is by Teodor Bok

After the Burroughs event, David received a sizeable grant from the Danish Ministry of Culture and founded an organization known as This World Poetry Foundation and invited me to sit on its board. He organized a three-day literary festival in the Betty Nansen Theater with international names like Amiri Baraka, Ken Kesey, Ed Sanders, Michael McClure, and the Fugs as well as many prominent Danish writers—Dan Turèll, Klaus Rifbjerg, Bo Green Jensen, Pia Tafdrup, Ib Michael, and others.

Poster from This World Poetry Festival 1984 where, inter alia, the readers included Ken Kesey, Ed Sanders, Michael McClure, Amiri Baraka and many others

Since then and since Bodil's untimely death at the age of 46 and David's departure to Amsterdam, I have had very infrequent contact with the Booktrader, but today I am on my way to learn about the more recent history of the store and to learn more about Lars Rasmussen. Moving against the stream, I thread through the demonstrators marching along Skindergade toward the Town Hall. I snap a couple of photographs in passing and am rewarded with the devil sign by the young marchers—learning only later that this is the contemporary equivalent of flashing the okay circle of finger and thumb.

Sidling down the three steps into the shop, I find Lars—despite his Dostoevskian appearance—not a brooding fellow, but a smiling, welcoming host. In no time at all he is filling me in on the shop, its history before him, its history with him, its current history. He is also filling glasses with an excellent Chilean merlot.

I learn that Lars lives in the little north side neighborhood of Brønshøj, near the marshes, with his wife, Birte, who managed the other bookshop (The Magic Flute) he opened in eastern Copenhagen for a few years in the '90s.

Formally educated as an antiquarian, Lars explains that there are those who deal with rare books and those who handle ordinary second hand volumes. He describes himself primarily as the latter, although he does deal in some rare books. When he has something very expensive, he auctions it on line. He tells about the history of the building that houses The Booktrader, built in 1831-32 on the ruins of the old Grey Friar Monastery (Gråbrodrekloster), which was demolished in 1536, during the Reformation. Excavations in the backyard indicate that people, possibly monks, had been buried here during the Middle Ages. Skindergade is one of the oldest streets in Copenhagen, originally housing the city's skin and fur traders. Around 1880 it was host to ten bookstores, four of them dealing exclusively with used books. Today only one other remains on the street in addition to the Booktrader.

Under David Grubb, the store sold only English books. Lars Rasmussen's stock is half Danish, half English, and he deals only in the humanities, specializing in fiction, poetry, history, art, architecture, photography, linguistics, philosophy, psychology, religion, literary criticism and music (jazz, blues and rock). The store also hosts occasional exhibitions of sculpture and art.

Our conversation by the counter is interrupted by customers. One asks if Lars has any Modesty Blaise in stock, and after he has directed her to the relevant shelf, he says to me with a smile, "You won't include that, will you?" A man comes in to ask for books about glass, of which Lars has none at the moment. I learn that books on glass are few and far between. A woman wants something on Chaucer. Lars collects two armloads from different sections of the store and lays them out for her on a stone sculpture that doubles as a display table. After much deliberation and some advice from Lars that she might be able to find precisely what she wants at a shop just up from Nytorv, she leaves without buying a thing. Lars seems undiscouraged, even when the next customer asks in German for a book about clock mechanisms.

Another man enters and requests one of the Joyces in the window. I ask if he is a Joycean, but he seems disinclined to reply. Yet another man steps down the three stairs to talk about the shoddy work that has been done on the cobblestones just outside. Lars tells him he's worried that someone might trip, and the man promises to do something about that as he stands with his head tilted back to admire the erotic sculpture overhead. When he is gone, I ask, "Who was that?"

Lars looks at me. "I don't know."

At just that moment a man in suit and tie enters and presents Lars with a half quart can of Guinness stout. Lars thanks him and the man wanders off to browse through the shelves.

I recall that David Grubb once told me he had to bring in an average of a thousand crowns a day (about $150) to stay in business.

"It's more like 2½ times that now," says Lars.

His lease on the shop expired some time ago so he is at the mercy of the landlord who increased his rent last year by forty thousand crowns (about $6,500) and there is an automatic increase of 5% a year.

The door opens again and Greg and Birgit Stephenson appear.

After a flurry of hugs, we reminisce about the old days, the three-day festival with the Fugs singing their '60s hit, "I Feel Like a Bowl of Home-made Shit," and Ken Kesey drinking beer and snorting stuff and making a carny event of bending the bottle caps double between thumb and forefinger. I remember being disappointed at his reading —a two-dimensional portrait of John Lennon, caricatures of good and evil that he seemed to want to believe, a writer whose first two novels in the 60s had revised my mind. But in retrospect, I am immensely grateful to have had the opportunity to meet him, for his good cheer, for the opportunity to hang around with him and Ed Sanders and the others. On that occasion I also had the opportunity to ask Kesey, during a press conference, whether he would be willing to participate in a literary wrestling match with John Irving since both writers had been college wrestling champs. Kesey looked coolly at me and said, "I would drink John Irving like a glass of water."

The editors of *Pearl* (from left): Lars Rasmussen, Gregory Stephenson, Birgit Stephenson. Note alphabet of books above and to the right

Greg Stephenson is the author of several books of literary criticism – studies of J. G. Ballard (*Out of the Night* and *Into the Dream*), Gregory Corso (*Exiled Angel*), the beat generation (*The Daybreak Boys*) and *Understanding Robert Stone*. When I ask what he is writing now, he answers with his mild voice and expression, which have always seemed to me mildly and blithely ironic, "Nothing. I don't have time to write or to read either—only teach. I've got two part-time jobs at Copenhagen University which take me 11-12 hours a day seven days a week."

We try to remember the names of all the people who used to gravitate around the Booktrader, the group of regulars who would assemble at Charlie's (then Charlie's Wine Room under the original eponymous Charlie, an Englishman who turned a failing bookshop into a thriving public house), but it has been a couple of decades—Martin Benson, the Scottish painter; the late John Fowlie, a British photographer and artist whose ungrounded imprisonment on false drug charges inspired a story of mine called "Danish Light"; Barry De George from Los Angeles, who had been writing a doctoral dissertation at Lund University asserting that the oil crisis of 1973 was a sham (*Interpreting Crises*) while fighting a legal battle to claim his Italian passport so he could move to Rome. There was an enormous young Dutch guy who had been a paratrooper in the Amazon, a sea captain who had hosted Thanksgiving for the whole group...

Soon Greg and Birgit are on their way, and Lars is popping the cork of another bottle of Chilean. A man who responds to an empty bottle by opening another is my kind of fellow, and the interview plunges on.

I ask if he has plans for more events, readings. Although people are eager for him to do so, he says, there really isn't enough room in the shop. This is why he started the CD series instead. There are twenty-three of them with some of the best living writers in Denmark, perhaps in northern Europe. Poets like Henrik Nordbrandt and Pia Tafdrup, both of whom have won the Nordic Literature Prize over the past few years, the highest honor that can be bestowed on a Scandinavian short of the Nobel; Inger Christensen, highly celebrated in Europe though little known in the English-speaking world. The recently deceased Thorkild Bjørnvig, whose infamous apprenticeship to Karen Blixen (yes—the one played by Meryl Streep) is celebrated in the book *The Pact*.

As if on cue, a young woman comes down to ask for Inger Christensen's CD. "She has such a wonderful voice," the girl says, and Lars rings up 125 crowns (about $20).

"Do the CDs support themselves," I ask.

Matter of factly, he replies, "Not at all. A few of them have sold about ten copies."

"Do you give a discount if someone buys all twenty-three."

"It could happen."

Another customer enters, bearing a satchel. Lars glances at him and says, "See what I have." Clearly he knows the man's passion. Lars disappears into a side room and re-emerges with a large, hard-bound book that he lays open, flat, on the center table. It is an 1850 edition of a German toy catalogue. The man leafs slowly through the book. "These illustrations are hand-painted," he murmurs. "I don't even dare ask the price." Lars explains that you can date the catalogue by looking at the illustration of the toy steam engine, an early model, and they get to discussing the dating of books. From a folder in his satchel, his customer takes out a large sheet of paper on which are printed all the varieties of the Penguin logo from its first appearance until now – there are penguins at attention, dancing penguins, hopping penguins, waddling penguins. Lars agrees to print the sheet with some commentary by the customer in his next Christmas Album.

Among the books Lars has published are one about the German artist, George Grosz, a couple of his own collections of whimsical erotic stories under a pseudonym (he has also written several hundred pages of short stories for which he is seeking an American publisher), a few books about South African jazz, even one about golf because one of his daily customers is a golfer.

"Do you play golf yourself?"

"Not at all. It would bore me to death. But this golfer architect came in every day, and I got the idea to publish his articles, and we sold the whole edition of 800 copies. That was our only success. The jazz books had their initial inspiration because in the '60s and '70s a lot of African jazz musicians started coming to Copenhagen to get away from the apartheid. At that time, we didn't really have racism. That came later. They played at Montmartre, and that's where I first heard them and was so attracted I started collecting their records. The first book I did on this was a discography of Dollar Brand or Abdullah Ibrahim as he is now known—a huge book—and that led to a book about his wife, the singer, Bea Benjamin. Then I stumbled over an amazing collection of historical photographs of jazz musicians from Cape Town from the 60s taken by a German guy named Hardy Stockmann. I traced him to Bangkok and bought his whole collection of pictures and published it. After the sixth book, I had to stop. The financial side of it was terrible—big books with pictures, very expensive, and they don't sell much. But making them was fun. There is still a stock available."

Display of Booktrader publications on South African jazz and golf. "Do you play golf yourself, Lars?" "Not at all. It would bore me to death."

Lars is in Cape Town once a year to hear jazz. He avoids Johannesburg which is very rough, but has never felt threatened in Cape Town or the townships. "In Cape Town you still see white people traveling first class on the trains and black people in third class. Even at some of the beaches that used to be white only, it is rare to see black people.

And sometimes a black person will call you 'boss'—from the Dutch 'baas'—but basically those are people trying to sell you something, to flatter you."

"But the jazz clubs are good?"

"There are a few jazz clubs in Cape Town. They come and go, but I especially like to hear the old guys play. Local style Cape Town jazz influenced by a lot of things, tribal music, but also an interesting influence from Malay music because there is a Malaysian population in Cape Town who were brought there as slaves, and they have their own music which has influenced the jazz. So Cape Town jazz is unique. I got to meet a lot of people because I was never afraid to go into the townships—a lot of white people are afraid to go there—but I never had any trouble at all. I take a lot of pictures of those guys, too."

He also visits New York every year and stays at a hotel on 17th between Fifth and Sixth Avenues called the Chelsea Inn (no relation to the Chelsea Hotel), a small place run by very nice people where, he says, you can get a nice double for about $140.

Another of Lars's specialties is the beat generation. He is currently preparing a Burroughs catalogue, has a good collection of Burroughs photos that have never been shown before anywhere, and they will be for sale. He also has many books by the beats. He has built up his stock in the shop from scratch; when David moved out the shop was empty. He had sold every last book.

One thing that he does continue to publish is his annual Christmas Album—a collection of writing and art solicited from his customers, some of whom are professionals, others amateurs. He has been publishing this annually since 1990, except for three years when he didn't have the money. He sees it as a kaleidoscope of styles and sensibilities, and he gives the magazine away free, with ten copies for each contributor. It is published on December 3rd every year, the birthday of the classic Danish writer, Ludvig Holberg, whose seated sculpture sits outside the Royal Theater on the King's New Square. People come in to the shop that day to pick up their copies. "We have a lot of fun that day," Lars says.

"Perhaps some come with wine also?"

"It happens," he says. "If I get a bit drunk I can tell you stories. Now that we're starting to talk about that, they're coming back to me. Next time you're here, I'll tell you some stories." But he goes on now anyway.

BOOKTRADER'S CHRISTMAS ALBUM 2004
15th Edition – still the nation's only infantile-psychotic Christmas Album
Edited by Lars Rasmussen

Booktrader Christmas Album—a collection of writing and art edited by Lars Rasmussen and solicited from his customers, some of whom are professionals, others amateurs, a kaleidoscope of styles and sensibilities. The magazine is published on December 3rd every year, the birthday of the classic Danish writer, Ludvig Holberg.

In the first half of the 90s, he tells me, his shop became a wild place. When he opened at eleven, people showed up with beer and wine and would have a couple of drinks. They would leave and then the next group would come in and then the next. But Lars was there with each group, drinking all day until he closed—as many as twenty bottles of beer a day. It was great fun and very exciting. People were drinking, smoking, fucking in the back room. Books fell onto the floor. People would dance on them. Books were thrown out the door onto Skinner Street. People laughed and cheered and opened fresh beers. There was a woman who when she came in sometimes would remove her blouse and walk around topless as long as she was there. Lars and his wife had separated, and he was often sleeping in the back of the shop, on the floor, no mattress.

"It was great."

He was in his forties. Everyone who came in for the daily party was free to leave at will, but he was a captive guest. Not that he didn't like it. He liked it. The guests were fun and interesting and many of them were famous as well. But at one point he realized that he was killing himself.

Finally one day he put up a no smoking sign. That cut the size of the daily party in half. Then he cut down drastically on his own drinking. People had begun to see him as the host, the joyous host, and when he was no longer throwing them back, the party began slowly to wind down. Then he had his life back again, and happily, he and his wife got back together again. But he never regretted those times. He thinks back on them even today with pleasure and nostalgia.

"You should have been here, Tom," he says, and I wish I had been, wish I had known.

Today, he and his wife live a stone's throw from their daughter and two grandchildren in a house they bought in the mid-1980s in the Brønshøj section, just north of Copenhagen. It occurs to me that in 2008, the Booktrader will have been in function for twenty-five years, and Lars will have been the proprietor for twenty of those years.

"That's a big event," I say. "You ought to do something to celebrate."

"Yes," he says, "Maybe I should burn the place down."

"Really," I say. "You should do something. We could fly David Grubb in for the event."

"Maybe," he says. "We'll see."

"Really. You should. I'll chip in for his ticket."

"Maybe so," he says. "Sure, why not, we could do that." He smiles enigmatically at me. "Maybe so."

"ANOTHER STUPID PARTY" Jane Austen and Bath

Walter Cummins

ALISON, MY WIFE, AND I arranged to spend some time in Bath, an opportunity to explore its wonders more fully than we had been able to previously in limited day trips. Even from the very first time we shared the reaction of a poet friend when she stood in the center of a panorama that takes in the Abbey, the Avon River, the Roman Baths, the Pump Room, and more. In awe, she exclaimed, "It's the most beautiful city I've ever seen." It's certainly hard to argue with that.

A Roman legacy and rows of Georgian buildings, some in arcs of crescents behind wide green lawns. The Pulteney Bridge crossing the Avon, crammed with tiny shops. The cascading waters of the weir. The parkland along the river's banks. An ambiance that even twenty-first century commerce cannot spoil.

For any literary traveler, it's impossible to pass even a few hours in Bath without thinking about Jane Austen. The city and its social role during her lifetime receive mention in each of her novels, sometimes just brief references but extensively in *Northanger Abbey* and with a central plot role in her last completed novel, *Persuasion*.

For me, finding echoes of Austen's Bath was one more step in a pilgrimage that had a gap of many years. I recall, decades before, walking down a street in Winchester and being surprised to find a plaque on the building where Jane had stayed and eventually died during her final months. That encounter took place not long after I had toured the Austen home in Chawton, now a museum open to visitors, and seen Jane's rooms and her writing table.

Bath does have a Jane Austen Centre, with memorabilia and a tearoom, at 40 Gay Street, not far from and similar to the house Jane, his sister Cassandra, and her mother occupied briefly at 25 Gay Street. The Centre is an emulation, not quite the real thing, lacking the authenticity of Chawton, but still providing the pleasures of a costume drama. Alison and I sought a more accurate experience.

Throughout our explorations, we found the past intermingled with the present. Our hotel, the Abbey on North Parade, stood next door to a Moroccan restaurant. A few steps to the corner and to the right on Pierrepont Street, Thai and Nepalese restaurants were just doors apart. What would Jane Austen have made of rajma curry, alu tareko, stuffed harchar, and khobj b'chehma? Her typical meal in the late 18th and early 19th centuries might have consisted of a pudding, white soup, mutton, or cold pork and mustard.

If Jane had, as we did, stepped from the door of our hotel—built in 1742 and in business during her time in Bath—and turned left to toward the Roman Baths and the Abbey, she would have been familiar with Sally's Lunn's house, the oldest extant building in the city, named for a French refugee who arrived in England and invented the Bath bun on the premises. Jane may have eaten a few of those, and she still could order a 21st-century version, allegedly smaller than the original. But, most likely, she would be befuddled by the French and vegetarian restaurants next door.

Many of the city's pubs probably existed during her time, though it's hard to imagine Jane Austen with a pint in her dainty hand, one much better suited for writing novels of great social insight and wit.

Still, if not the cuisine, the overall architecture of the city would have been very familiar to her—the Roman Baths, the Pump Room, the Abbey, the Pulteney Bridge, the Circus, and several blocks away, the impressive sweep of the Royal Crescent.

The Pump Room, where the Georgian elite gathered to display their finery, and which served as the site of scenes in *Northanger Abbey* and *Persuasion*, is today yet another Bath restaurant, albeit with more traditional food and a string ensemble entertaining the diners, almost all of whom eat in street clothes.

No doubt, it's the clothing that would have disoriented Jane more than any other phenomena in today's Bath—the look of the January visitors, gawking at the sites dressed in jeans, fleece or down jackets, and wool hats, backpacks slung over their shoulders. In Jane Austen's Bath people wouldn't have ventured out the door without assurance that they looked a la mode, emulating the heights of fashion, competing with the style setters. To be otherwise would have been a source of shame and even scandal.

Richard "Beau" Nash, the city's unofficial master of ceremonies and one responsible for its establishment as a center of society in the mid 18th century, also set new standards for the fashion of his time, wearing a black wig instead of the standard white, his white hat at a jaunty angle. His waistcoats were brocaded, his shifts ruffled. He became a leading arbiter of men's style throughout England, even with women seeking his advice. Not a waistcoat or ruffled shirt to be seen in today's Bath.

But they must have been common when people gathered in the Pump during Jane Austen's time. Now the Pump Room, next to the Roman Baths, with a bust of Nash in one niche, serves food and shares the Bath's mineral waters whose supposed curative power drew so many to the city in the 1700 and 1800s. A fountain in the restaurant flows with warm spa water that people flocked to drink in the past and some—a curious few—still do. Even choosing not to indulge, one can enjoy a meal to the music of the string trio and piano playing on a balcony suspended over the large room, the music accompanied by the tinkling of silverware on fine china.

As a center of Bath Society, the Pump Room went through several iterations from the time it was first built in 1706. The final version from 1796, the one that exists today, is eighty-five feet long, forty-six feet wide, and thirty-four feet high. This is the room depicted in a Rowlandson drawing of 1798.

Jane Austen herself knew Bath well firsthand. She lived in the city between 1801 and 1806, from ages 26 to 31, after her clergyman father retired from his parsonage at the village of Steventon. Jane, according to reports, was distraught at having to leave that home in a small Hampshire community and relocate to what she considered a crowded, oppressive city that lacked open countryside for walking.

Anne Elliott, the heroine of *Persuasion*, shares her author's opinion when she is relocated to Bath early in that novel: "But the usual fate of Anne attended her, in having something very opposite from her inclination fixed on. She disliked Bath, and did not think it agreed with her; and Bath was to be her home."

Later, returning to the city from the country, "She persisted in a very determined, though very silent disinclination for Bath; caught the first dim view of the extensive buildings, smoking in rain, without any wish of seeing them better ..." Of course, by the end of the novel it is in Bath where Anne renews her love with Captain Wentworth, which does compensate for the place. But that's fiction.

In an 1801 letter to her sister Cassandra, Jane Austen wrote: "Another stupid party last night; perhaps if larger they might be less intolerable, but here there were only just enough to make one card table, with six people to look over, & talk nonsense to each other."

That wasn't the worst of it. Her father, ill when he retired, died in January 1805, leaving family in financial need. Their residences in Bath became less and less fashionable, to the point where they could no longer remain. The first home was at 4 Sydney Place for a three-year lease; then they moved to 27 Green Park Buildings, where Jane's father died. Loss of his income made it necessary for Mrs. Austen and her daughters Jane and Cassandra to move to the Gay Street residence. Six months later they ended up on Trim Street, a narrow lane in the darker and much less desirable part of town.

Fortunately, in the summer of 1806, with the financial assistance of Jane's brothers, they left Bath permanently, moving first to Clifton and next Southampton. Jane was relieved to be out of Bath, which she probably liked even less after seeing her father die and the family's circumstances worsen. She wrote to Cassandra in 1808: "It will be two years tomorrow since we left Bath for Clifton, with what happy feelings of escape." In 1809, again with the help of brothers, the women relocated to a home in the village of Chawton, where Jane spent the final eight years of her short life.

Cassandra sketch of Jane

She actually died in 1817 at age 42 in Winchester, where she had travelled with Cassandra and her brother Henry to seek aid for a worsening disease that was never identified. She is buried in Winchester Cathedral. Upon Jane's death, Cassandra wrote to her friend Fanny Knight: "*I have lost a treasure, such a Sister, such a friend as never can have been surpassed,-She was the sun of my life, the gilder of every pleasure, the soother of every sorrow, I had not a thought concealed from her, & it is as if I had lost a part of myself."*

Her brother Henry said of her last days, "she supported, during two months, all the varying pain, irksomeness, and tedium," attendant on her decline "with more than resignation, with a truly elastic cheerfulness." "She retained," he says, "her faculties, her memory, her fancy, her temper, and her affections, warm, clear, and unimpaired, to the last . . . . She expired on Friday, July 18 (1817), in the arms of her sister."

For the millions who have read her novels, Jane Austen is very much alive, conveying unending "elastic cheerfulness." She did not "talk nonsense."

Several photographs are from Visit Bath. and others from the Internet. The oil of Beau Nash was painted by William Hoare.

LIQUIDATION OF THE HORSE THIEF
A scrap of war history in Copenhagen's Rosengårds Bodega

Thomas E. Kennedy

THERE IS A BULLET HOLE in the wall behind the bar at Rosengårds Bodega in Copenhagen. It has been there for over sixty years, put there during the Nazi occupation of this little north European country, a scrap of Danish history left over from the liquidation of a Gestapo snitch.

Bullet hole behind bar in Rosengårds Bodega—a bullet that missed the horse thief

Friends from Kansas City—Robert Stewart and Lisa Brown—are visiting us, so Alice and I invite them into the Bodega for a look. The owner is behind the bar, Niels Erik Nielsen, a tall trim man in his mid-fifties who has owned the place since 1977. When I ask if we might see the bullet hole, he moves aside a box of candles on a shelf and points at it. I know a bit about the story and begin to tell it when the owner catches my eye and throws his glance toward a table in the back. An old man sits there alone, nursing a bottle of porter, his dark blue maritime cap on the table beside him. He is not tall—maybe five-seven—and his grizzled hair and beard were clearly once red.

"Ask him about it," the owner suggests. "He was there."

We introduce ourselves and ask if we may join him, ask if he would like another porter, but he shakes his head. "One's my limit," he says. "I've had two heart operations."

We sit.

"What do you want to know?" he asks.

"The story of the bullet hole."

He is 81 years old, and his hearing is not good. We have to speak slowly and loudly into his right ear, and he can neither understand nor speak English, so I translate for Bob and Lisa. He can't understand my accent either, so Alice translates my Danish into Danish for him.

He says, "My involvement was completely coincidental. I had nothing to do with BOPA. I was on a job for Free Denmark." (BOPA and Free Denmark were two of the resistance groups in Denmark during the German occupation, 1940-45.) "I was mapping out the backyards here. Saboteurs needed to know how they could get through the backyards and out into another street after they had completed a job. Just as I came out in front of Rosengårds Bodega, two bicycles pulled up, one from each direction. I recognized the cyclists. One was Brandt. He was the leader of BOPA. The other was Martin, who was in charge of their Guard Group. Those aren't their real names, by the way. They're cover names."

"What's your name?" Alice asks.

"My name," he says, "is..." and makes a ring of his thumb and finger—a zero. "I was here by accident. I didn't shoot anybody. But Martin and Brandt knew me. I was an errand boy for a radio man. I was seventeen. Red-haired and freckle-faced and between the freckles a lot of ugly pimples. I looked ridiculous. That was good. I made sure I kept looking ridiculous so nobody looked twice at me when I was on an errand. That day I had just sketched the backyard behind the Bodega, and Martin and Brandt motioned me over. They called me Sleepy. We were just kids, and they picked our cover names from the Disney film, *Snow White*—the dwarves. I was 'Sleepy.'"

The Horse Thief (a.k.a. Rudolf Christiansen), Gestapo informer, liquidated on Hitler's 56th birthday

He pauses, remembering, sips his porter.

"We know from other sources that the two assassins had been following the Horse Thief all day. It was April 20, 1944, Hitler's fifty-fourth birthday. A present for the *führer*—the liquidation of a Gestapo informer. The Horse Thief's real name was Rudolf Christiansen and he himself was fifty years old. His nickname was conferred upon him by drinking companions when he bragged about a three-month sentence in Hungary for stealing a horse. The Royal Hungarian Horse Thief, they called him. He claimed to be a lot of things, but during the occupation he was on a payroll for fifteen hundred crowns a month—more money than a high-ranking civil servant made then—for information that could be useful to the Gestapo. That day a number of men from the underground shadowed him around Copenhagen from serving house to serving house, but in every one of them there was the risk of taking bystanders with him. At one point, he met a girl and they walked together through Ørsteds Park

"Martin and Brandt got off their bikes and asked me if I knew who the Horse Thief was. I knew him. He was a tall, skinny guy from a little fishing town, Dragør, in the south of Amager. He always wore this strange jacket. He used to find out things and pass them on to the Gestapo. Things that cost lives. That got people tortured. So they sent me in to Rosengårds Bodega—it was called Rosengårds Wine Room then—to see if the Horse Thief was there. I went in and started checking the ashtrays for cigarette butts. That's what we did then, collected butts and salvaged whatever tobacco was left to roll later. The place was full of people and smoke, but no one thought it was strange that this pimply kid came in checking ashtrays for butts. The Horse Thief was in there all right, sitting at the bar, his back to the door. I came out and told Martin and Brandt, and they said, Watch our bikes. Bikes were scarce then and would be stolen just like that. So I held the bikes, and they went in and pulled out their shooters..."

"What kind of guns?"

"I don't know. Probably 9 mm. A 9mm did the job. An 11 mm would drop an elephant. You know an 11 mm is the size of a Colt .45. You see John Vayne in the cowboy films twirling a Colt .45 around his finger. You know what a Colt .45 weighs—without the bullets? It weighs about eight pounds. I fired one once—I thought my arm was broken. You don't want to twirl that around your finger."

Another pause, another sip of porter, his blue eyes reflective behind his eyeglasses, before he continues.

"The first shot drove a furrow through the wood of the bar—not the bar that's there now, the old one—and planted itself in the wall. It's still there. There were a lot of shots. One report says seven, another eleven, but at least one bullet hit the Horse Thief in the head. They say he screamed like a pig, leaped up and tried to get his gun out, but his arm wouldn't help him. He fell to the right, off the stool. He was still making noise so they shot him twice in the chest. The bar got very quiet, but no one looked, no one saw anything. Martin and Brandt covered themselves with their pistols as they backed out. They were nervous. They weren't killers. It was their first liquidation. They grabbed their bikes and jumped on and rode smack into each other, fell down, the bikes clattered to the cobblestones. They got up and they were gone. That's the story. I didn't do anything. I watched the bikes, that's all. I was on a job to sketch the backyards. It was 1944. I was 17 years old, a pimply kid. I looked ridiculous.

The bar at Rosengårds Bodega today—tended by Danielle. the customer is seated to the left of where the Horse Thief sat when he was shot down

Bob suggests that Lisa take a photograph of Sleepy, but he holds up his palm. "No pictures."

We look at him. He smiles. "A man with an anonymous face is a safe man."

"But surely after all this time..."

His blue eyes fix on mine. "Not so long ago someone knocked on my door. Two men. They said, So and so sent us. I said, Rubbish. So and so is dead. I went to his funeral myself. They said, Then you know who we are. So I invited them in. They said, We've read your papers, and we have a question for you. Who was 'Ragpick' the code name for? They had my papers. They knew everything else. There was no point not to tell them. So I told them. They said, That's all we wanted to ask you. I told them I had a question. I wanted to know where my papers were. They had disappeared. I'd written everything down, all of it, and it had disappeared. I asked them where my papers were, and they said, What a stupid thing to ask, and they left. So that's why. It's never done with. I'm watched. I don't like being photographed."

"Sleepy" on Danish Liberation Day outside the Nimbus motorcycle factory in Copenhagen, where he worked and was a member of a resistance group during the German occupation of Denmark (1940-45). In the picture he is carrying a US carbine. He was 18 years old

From his inner jacket pocket he takes out what appears to be a blue plastic check book, but which apparently serves as his wallet. From it, he removes a small photocopy of a photograph. He writes something on the back and shoves it across the table to me. In the picture, a young man stands outside the Nimbus motorcycle factory wearing a beret and plus fours and holding a rifle. I look closely at the young man's features. Unmistakably it is Sleepy—the same nose and forehead and cheekbones and eyes. On the back he has written "5 May 1945" (Danish liberation day) and "Sleepy" and "US carbine." Clearly he is proud of the American rifle. He holds it in both hands, bore pointed obliquely toward the ground. He is sort of smiling, but the smile is a little bit grim, a little bit sardonic. Undeniably a young man who has seen some things. He by no means looks ridiculous. I would not like to stand up against him.

"You can keep that," he says. "I was eighteen years old. No one would ever recognize me now. In the Nimbus factory I was an apprentice. I had to address the guys who were already mechanics formally, by their last name. But at night we had a resistance group and there we were all on first name basis. The hardest part was to remember during the day not to use their first names. That would be a tip off."

Another sip of porter moistens his vocal chords. "The last half year of the occupation, I was an errand boy for a radio man, and I could see out the back door of his place to the King's Palace. Until the day he died I knew the Crown Prince, Frederick IXth, whose father was King Christian Xth, a real Nazi hater—when the Jews were ordered to wear arm bands, he put one on and rode on his horse through the city; he was later called the King of Freedom. When Frederick and I were alone together we were on first name basis. But I always treated him with respect. Later in my life, I became a train engineer, and I had Frederick with me in the locomotive. He loved trains." He smiles, the memory light in the blue of his eyes, glinting behind his lenses. Then he slides another photograph from his checkbook wallet. A young man seated on a motorcycle. Sleepy.

"That's taken in 1950," he says. Sleepy would have been twenty-three then. "And that's a Nimbus motorcycle, but it's a '24 model."

I turn the picture over and look at the back. A name is printed there. Sleepy's eyes become alert. Quickly he takes the picture from me. But not before I read the name. Bob saw it, too. He says quietly—too quietly for Sleepy to hear—"You'll take that name to your grave with you." I nod.

Bob asks, "Did your parents know about your underground activities?"

"They knew I was doing something, but they didn't ask any questions. Once I came home with a bullet hole in my plus fours. My mother patched it without a word. My one brother was underground in Jutland—he helped liberate the prisoners from Horsens jail. My other brother had a Nazi wife. It wasn't easy for my parents. I could tell you stories but it will have to wait until I'm dead." He smiles. "Then they can publish my papers. It's all written down. Whoever has them. If they haven't been sucked up by the vacuum-cleaner."

Suddenly he remembers something too good to resist. "Once I was up around Værløse, north of Copenhagen. There was an airfield there. I went into a local tavern where a lot of things happened, you know? I had my knapsack with me, and I put it down on the floor beside my chair, and the owner came over and said it didn't look nice to have my knapsack there and said he'd put it in the kitchen for me. So I knew he was going to put something into it—for me to deliver. The place was full of German officers. Nice enough guys. We were all singing together, and then it was time for me to go back to Copenhagen and the owner gave me my knapsack, and it was heavier than it had been before. The German officers were about to drive back to Copenhagen, too, and offered me a ride. They were okay. They knew they had to drop me on the edge of town because I couldn't be seen in a German vehicle—it would be the end of me. So I slung on my knapsack, and as we were leaving, the owner said, "Don't forget to eat your candy."

"What did that mean?"

He looks at me, thinking. "When I became an errand boy, I had to turn in my shooter. A .765. Instead of a receipt, they gave me a glass capsule full of cyanide. Hard candy. I was not to be taken alive." He thinks about that for a while before continuing. "But it was okay. I believed in God. I was deeply religious. I was ready to die."

Alice asks, "Are you still deeply religious?"

He shakes his head. "Religion and war go hand in hand all the way back in time. Back in Spain, they used to ask if you wanted to be baptized or preferred to have your head chopped off."

"So now you believe in yourself," Alice says.

He chuckles. "Not much of that left to believe in. No," he says, "the next war will be different for me. Last time I did what I thought was right, but they come after you later. They read your papers and they have questions. They watch you. It's never over. Next time, I'll just sit back and go for this." He rubs his thumb and forefinger together, laughing. "Just this."

But the blue of his eyes tells another story. He'd been a kid called on to do some hard things, and he did them. I look again at the picture of him standing in front of the Nimbus factory holding the carbine, his high cheekbones, slitted eyes, that smile that was not quite a smile.

"The radio man told me," he says, "Don't ever brag about this stuff. Stay anonymous. But he's dead, and no one knew about all that he did so I went and told his story to the war museum. And I told them about the bullet hole in the wall here, too, and gave them a picture of it. And that bullet hole is protected now. No one is allowed to fill it in. And no one has."

Rosengårds Bodega today. The bicycle to the right belongs to barmaid Danielle—not to an assassin

Bibliography

Brandt, Børge, and Christiansen, Kaj, *Sabotage*. Copenhagen: TIDEN Publishers, 1945, Chapter 13, pages 137-42 (in Danish).

Kennedy, *Thomas E., Kerrigan's Copenhagen, A Love Story*. Galway, Ireland: Wynkin de Worde Publishers, 2002, Chapter 19, pages 147-50.

A GRAND ILLUSION
Haut-Koenigsbourg

Walter Cummins

If you wanted to make a movie about war, what setting with more frisson than a castle, especially one with a long history of conquest and destruction, and an ultimate—for the time being—renewal?

For centuries castles served as symbols of power and dominance and served as fortifications to protect and control, to repel invaders and to extort tribute from those who lay vulnerable on the landscape below. Today they are relics, historical curiosities, objects d'art, tourist destinations for visitors treading the stone floors, swarming the parapets, peering through the ramparts. Now castles seem playthings, massive toys conveying the impression of a time long ago. Now they would be useless in warfare. A suicide bomber could demolish a castle in seconds, its thick walls disintegrated into a heap of rubble.

The director Jean Renoir, son of the painter, must have been conscious of the disparities between ancient and modern warfare when he chose the Alsatian castle of Haut-Koenigsbourg as a setting for a World War I German prison in his 1937 film, *La grande illusion.* Midway through the movie, a group of French officers, on the very day they had planned an escape from their original place of captivity, are ordered to be relocated to this castle, which serves as the unnamed stand-in for the fortress of Poméranie, an actual site of imprisonment for French soldiers.

Even though the filming of *La grande illusion* just precedes the Nazi savagery of the war to come, it is anachronistic in its depiction of the polite civility between captors and captured, with hands shaken, salutes given, and rules applied. Perhaps because his first audience knew what really happened in the First World War, Renoir does not refer to the futile butchery of trench warfare, the thousands slaughtered for a few yards of land. All that remains an unstated backstory.

These French prisoners, the viewer knows, are fortunate to be away from the battlefield, in rooms where they drink cognac shipped from Paris and dine on meals superior to those of their German captors. They receive a trunk of female fashions to dress in drag and perform a variety show backed by their own orchestra. They are on a first name basis with their guards. Given the bloody alternatives, it's not a bad life.

Yet they want to escape, not because of unpleasant conditions, but because escape is expected of them. It's what one does when held prisoner, an assumed obligation. Neither the French nor the Germans seem aware of the causes and goals of the war, the geopolitical aspirations of those who initiated the conflict. For them it's not unlike a World Cup match. You root for your side and do what's expected of you. Nothing you inflict on your enemy is personal or an act of animosity. Even if you have to shoot and kill, you do it because you are supposed to as one of the—to use the title of another Renoir film, "rules of the game." As officers on both sides say, "A duty is a duty."

That's exactly what happens when the aristocratic de Boeldieu creates a diversion by having the guards chase him as he climbs up the wooden steps to the top of the castle so that two other prisoners—the commoner, Maréchal, and the nouveau riche Jew, Rosenthal—can lower themselves down a stone wall with a makeshift rope and disappear into the countryside. When de Boeldieu refuses to stop, the German officer in charge, von Rauffenstein, de Boeldieu's well-born counterpart, must shoot a man he likes and respects, grieving at his deathbed.

The Great Room as seen in the movie

The Great Room in the present

After the hardships of crossing Alpine snows, Maréchal and Rosenthal find relief in an idyllic respite with a German woman widowed by the war and her blue-eyed little girl—even constructing a Christmas crèche from scraps. But they know they "must" cross into the neutrality of Switzerland.

Before this escape, Maréchal and the widow fall in love, he leaving reluctantly, she agreeing with his obligation, he promising to return to bring her and the child to Paris, if he lives. On the verge of crossing the Swiss border, it is Rosenthal who gives voice to the film's title when he says that once out of Germany their next goal will be to get back to their military units and into the war itself. He calls the journey of their escape an illusion, and by implication, war the reality.

But is it? For millions between 1914 and 1918, between 1939 and 1945, and many thousands in the world today, war was and is the reality, not love between a French man and a German woman, not the joy of a child's delight, not a fine meal with excellent cognac. Yet the battlefields of European wars are now reborn with new growth, the cities rebuilt, the past bombardments subjects for History Channel documentaries. Haut-Koenigsbourg, site of a millennium of battles and bodies, revitalized as a monument, welcomes visitors, the most popular tourist destination in Alsace.

Alsace and its neighboring province of Lorraine have become symbols of a dominant reason for warfare over the centuries—the conquest and possession of territory. Placed between France and Germany, the region has endured a long history of conquest and re-conquest. Beginning in 921, it spent several hundred years as a territory of the Holy Roman Empire, but was annexed by France with the 1648 Peace of Westphalia. Two centuries later, after the Franco-Prussian War of 1871, it became part of the new German Empire. The allied victory in the First World War led to a very brief period of independence. On the same day the Armistice was signed, November 11, 1918, local citizens proclaimed the Republic of Alsace-Lorraine. But within a week French troops began occupying the main cities, and the region was officially returned to France by the Treaty of Versailles.

With the march of the Nazi Wehrmacht at the start of World War II, Alsace and Lorriane were annexed by Germany in 1940. Residents of military age were drafted into the German military, and some even volunteered. That led to recriminations at the end of the war, when the French once again took control, along with official repression of the German dialect spoken in the region, where many of the family and place names are clearly Germanic.

Towering over the Alsatian plain, Haut-Koenigsbourg castle has endured literal ups and downs since it was first built in the late 12th century, reduced to a ruin in the 17th century, abandoned for two hundred years, and reconstructed at the beginning of the 20th by Kaiser Wilhelm of Germany. Its prospect gives the castle a view of miles in many directions -- the Rhine valley, the Black Forest, and the Vosges mountains, an ideal advantage for a fortification built to control the countryside.

The initial structure on the site was a Teutonic castle built by the Swabian Emperor Frederick of Hohenstaufen in 1114. The first destruction took place in 1462 by a force from the upper Rhine cities. The Hapsburg family assumed ownership in 1454. In 1479, the counts of Thiestein rebuilt and modernized for artillery weapons. In 1633, during the Thirty Year War when the Swedes conquered Alsace, they took the castle after a three-month siege. Haut Koenigsbourg was destroyed again, first ransacked and then burned. This time it stayed a ruin for the next two centuries, with only a few large rooms preserved. With Germany back in control of the province, in 1899 the castle was given to Emperor Wilhelm II, the much-despised (by the Allies) Kaiser of World War I.

Though it hardly makes up for the death and destruction for which he was responsible, Wilhelm did undertake the restoration of the castle as part of his plans to re-Germanize Alsace. Under the supervision of the architect Bodo Ebhardt, a specialist in medieval fortification who was guided by archeological evidence, the project took eight years. On the second floor, the vault of the Kaiser's Hall displays the imperial eagle next to the Prussian motto, and the hall houses the

the imperial eagle next to the Prussian motto, and the hall houses the Hohenzollern family coat of arms. Wilhelm was making a statement, one that contributed to the outbreak of World War I. During the Nazi occupation of Alsace during World War II, the castle became the hiding place of art treasures from museums and cathedrals in Colmar and Strasbourg.

Between the wars, Jean Renoir used Haut-Koenigsbourg as a set. One commentator on *La grande illusion* notes that the director's "perennial concern is with boundaries that keep people apart and the possibility of transcending them." It's not just people but also the boundaries between conflict and connection, between war and peace, between what is normal and what is aberration.

Now, in a time of peace throughout Europe, the historic past of Haut-Koenigsbourg seems unreal. Why would invaders want to destroy such a magnificent structure? Why would people who have no personal animus use it to imprison someone who speaks a different language and favors a different cuisine? So much of what actually happened feels like the makebelieve of a movie. Doesn't it?

AIRPORTS, HOTELS, TAXICABS

Thomas E. Kennedy

He traveled here, he traveled there—
But not the value of a hair
Was heart or head the better.
—William Wordsworth

When I was a kid, we never went anywhere. We never even moved. Not once. I was dying to see the world beyond my little neighborhood in New York City, and as soon as I could, I started making forays into it. Let the footloose midwesterners and southerners dream of being a part of N'Yawk N'Yawk. The midwest, the south, the southwest, the west, the northwest called to me like distant arabies, as did the shores beyond. I hitchhiked, rode buses, took planes when I could manage the fare. I loved traveling. It seemed like a nowhere that was everywhere, no longer where you were, not yet where you would be, a suspension of time on a Trailways or Greyhound bus watching America roll past, people getting on and off, different people, with their duffel bags and cardboard suitcases, unknown tales etched into their faces

With this penchant, it was probably inevitable I would find a job that involved travel, which led to an international post and relocation to Europe, first to France, then to Denmark, where the travel accelerated quantumly. I traveled constantly, a day or two at a time, sometimes two or three times a week. Sometimes I would fly out in the morning for a luncheon meeting and fly back again in the afternoon. Once I flew from Copenhagen to Chicago for a dinner meeting, then back early next morning. Another time, I traveled some 30 hours from Copenhagen to Sydney for a one-day meeting and back again.

Sometimes I traveled alone, but usually with others, often a group, to meetings and conferences. Those who do not travel in their work tend to call such trips "junkets," implying that they lack seriousness, but in fact, usually the work was not easy and the pleasures few. There were papers to read and analyse, strategies to prepare, research, position papers and reports, resolutions and statements to draft. Often, instead of lunch, we had strategy sessions, the brief coffee pauses were rife with lobbying, and in the evening "official" dinners dragged on with speeches delivered consecutively in three languages. There is little more tiring than sitting in a conference room for an eight-hour day, listening attentively to presentations, taking notes, hurrying to put on your earphones for the simultaneous interpretation when someone takes the floor and begins speaking French, Italian, Greek, German, Spanish, Portuguese ... Listening through earphones to interpreters, sometimes for hours, is vaguely surreal. The interpreters' contract ensures that they get regular breaks every half hour or so from their strenuous activity; the meeting participants are extended no such mercy. Sometimes, rendering the speaker's emotion, the interpreter will suddenly shout, snarl, accuse, drip sarcasm, giving the listener a jolt: Who is this stranger, this disembodied voice, snarling into my inner ear? People who forget they are wearing earphones shout comments to their neighbors that are intended to be sly, whispered confidences, and chairpersons who forget to screen their mikes for a moment's private, indiscrete relief have their indiscretions interpreted into a couple of hundred ears in half a dozen languages.

Even the best interpreters are faced with a near impossible task, often attempting to render incoherency in one language coherent in another. Once, as a Greek speaker ranted at some length from the podium, the head of my delegation, Jesper Poulsen, began looking around at the simultaneous-interpretation cabins in exasperation, as if to ask, who is doing this incoherent translation, and the woman responsible snapped over the headphones, "Dammit, Dr Poulsen, it doesn't make any sense to me either!"

Traveling much, the memory fails, details melt together, dissolve. It becomes harder to remember anything of it all. I can say cheers in Irish, French, German, Estonian, Russian, Polish, Chinese, Japanese and two ways in Finnish. I can curse in Finnish and Swedish, request the check from a waiter or a receipt from a cab driver in German, French and Scandinavian, order a beer in French, Spanish, German and Danish and a beer, snaps and fried foreleg of pig in Cologne. But in what more than superficial way has that enriched me? The travel grows routine, hotels grow boring—even the most luxurious five-star becomes a dull, lonely place, like the magnificent quarters in which Keir Dulea dies in *2001, A Space Odyssey.* What did I actually see in Barcelona, what did I experience in Tokyo, in Hong, in Budapest? How had I lived up to the fulfilled dreams of travel from my childhood?

One day, after I had been trotting the globe for nearly twenty-five years, someone said to me, "You've had such an exciting life. You must have seen just about everything!"

And I thought, *Yes, I've seen the airports and hotels and taxicabs of a hundred cities, two hundred!* In truth, aside from a few handfuls of sights, I might as well have been attending meetings anywhere, nowhere—like the conferences that were sometimes arranged for us in Frankfurt airport so everyone could fly in and out without having even to glimpse the city.

What I had most wanted to do with my life was write, but for most, writing does not provide economic stability for a family; I didn't want my children to suffer as a result of my graphomania. So, like many writers, I lived two lives, but throughout my business life, I wrote as much as I could while saving money with the aim of being able to write full-time when I turned sixty. The realization of how poorly I had used the excellent opportunities of travel which had been mine for a quarter century came less than a decade before my sixtieth birthday.

On the other hand, in addition to the demanding work, I also had some fun, often demanding fun. There were exotic dinners and lunches that required a stretch of the gut and a tolerance for wines of many colors as well as pre- and post-prandial spirits, and occasionally the conference organizer treated us to a brief tour of some local sight or event: Bullfights in Madrid, Flamenco dances in Barcelona, Fado singers in a Porto café, monks swinging from churchbell ropes in Santiago de Compostela, a strip club in Luxembourg, a *Bateau Mouche* dinner tour on the Seine where at a specific moment our French hosts had arranged for a line of their office colleagues to turn around, drop their pants and moon us from the bank, an offer to wrestle the half-grown calfs in the northern Spanish countryside outside Segovia followed by Sopa Castellana afloat with pigs' ears at Mesón de Cándido, suckling baby pigs carved with the edge of a dish by Cándida, "the greatest inkeeper of Castilla," strolls on Helsinki's beautiful broad waterfront, watching the snow fall on the elegant town hall square in Tallinn or into the icy mouth of Turku's River Apu. And the occasional very rare treat—a safari in South Africa, a mountain tour in Uruguay or the Gap of Dunlo, a visit to Pablo Neruda's Isla Negra in Chile, or the Thousand Armed Buddha in Kyoto, a Geisha House in Tokyo (at a thousand dollars a nose), the Opera House in Sydney, a boat tour up the Chao Phraya river through Bangkok.

The seeming insatiable itch of my boyhood travel lust was being heartily scratched. Soon my passport needed a sheaf of new pages and those were filled and needed additions, and the list of cities I had visited, many of them several times, grew longer than both arms: Montevideo, Santiago, Isla Negra, London, Porto, Lisbon, Madrid, Barcelona, Segovia, Toledo, Seville, Santiago de Compostela, Cambridge, Athens, Amsterdam, Crete, Cyprus, Lesbos, Cephallonia, Lefkas, Rhodes, Cape Town, Helsinki, Turku, Dublin, Killarney, Waterford, Galway, Kong, Århus, Aalborg, Odense, Dunleary, Stockholm, Malmo, Alta, Oslo, Edinburgh, Glasgow, Ljubljana, Porta Rosa, Dubrovnik, Tashkent, Miyazaki, Bangkok, Hong Kong, Frankfurt, Hamburg, Berlin, East Berlin (before the wall came down), Cologne, Paris, Reykjavik, Stratford-on-Avon, Luxembourg, Baden-Baden, Strasbourg, Budapest, Malta, Madeira, Bali, Geneva, Lausanne, Basle, Zurich, Ferney-Voltaire, Venice, Firenza, Verona, Roma, Napoli, Sicily, Kyoto, Vienna, Brussels, Brussels, Brussels,Brussels....

The people I traveled with were fun. Often it was just myself and the president of my company, Jesper. He and I shared an affinity for vodka martinis and Shakespeare and spent many a night, after a hard day of conferences and negotiations (he negotiated, I took notes and offered the occasional nugget of advice), imbibing vodka martinis unto the wee hours and engaging in Shakespeare-quoting contests.

The game was to take turns offering quotes until one of us ran dry. I was a crack quoter of Eliot, Housman, and Thomas, less adept at the Bard. My offerings were generally the usual ones:

> You blocks, you stones, you worse than senseless things! O you hard hearts, you cruel men of Rome.
>
> O that this too too solid flesh would melt, thaw, resolve itself in dew...
>
> Tomorrow and tomorrow and tomorrow...

and so forth, while Jesper, who had sowed his wild oats as an actor in a street theater in London, had storehoused heaps of the less worn ones:

> Lie still, ye thief, and hear the Lady sing in Welsh.
> I had rather hear Lady, my bitch, howl in Irish.
>
> In England indeed they are most potent in potting. Your Dane, your German and your swag-bellied Hollander – Drink ho! – are nothing to your English. He drinks with facility your Dane dead drunk. He sweats not to overthrow your Almain. He gives your Hollander a vomit ere the next pottle can be filled.
>
> This is my right hand, and this is my left hand. I am not drunk now; I can stand well enough, and I speak well enough.
>
> Pardon the frankness of my mirth.
> I'll mentor you with my foot!
>
> Let me go, sir, or I'll knock you o'er the mazard!

Despite my degree in literature and my English mother-tongue (American, Brit colleagues would be quick to correct me), I always lost, my mazard was always emptied first, although the reports of the meeting negotiations that I wrote next day tended toward iambic pentameter.

We enjoyed our journeys and adventures. In South Africa, we were chased by two angry rhinoceri and stalked by two skinny (read, hungry) lions in the bush outside Kruger Park and drank vodka martinis by the fire that night while elephant silently circled our encampment – it is stunning how quietly an elephant can step over twigs or the stillness with which a huge herd of buffallo can hoof through the dusky bush to a water hole at sundown. In the Uruguayan mountains, we negotiated with a large, angry tarantula who had colonized Jesper's billfold, while our guide cowered behind us, murmuring, "Muy pelegroso! Muy pelegroso! They can jump, señor!"

Jesper is a physician by education, and I always felt secure traveling with him in the event some medical emergency might arise. He did in fact once, on the island of Malta, remove some stitches from my back, employing for the task a fingernail clipper sterilized in vodka.

My travel companion, Jesper—Dr Jesper Poulsen (left) at the unveiling of his portrait by Danish artist Peter Rothmeier Ravn (right). (Foto credit: Tommy Oesterlund.)

I also recall a late night in London where his alert sense of human nature saved me from making a fool of myself. We were in my hotel room having a last martini from the minibar—no doubt the last martini in the minibar—when I heard through the wall from the next room what I thought was a case of child abuse in progress. A woman with a cruel, crisp British accent was saying, "You are a very, very *naughty* little boy, and you shall have to be punished." I became irate and was about to rush out and holler through the door of the room, "Leave that child alone!" when Jesper smiled and said, "Maybe it's not really what you think."

Sometimes in our travels we were forced closer together than normally would be expected of two business colleagues. Arriving late at night in Athens once, we found that the conference hotel had only one room available—with a double bed. We decided to go out to the Plaka for a nightcap before retiring, and the nightcap became several. Next morning, as sometimes happens when you travel a lot, I woke up not certain where I was. Then I heard snoring beside me and looked to see the back of a very large male lying there and thought, "Oh Christ, what have I done this time!"

Because I had a writing vocation parallel to my business life, my journeys sometimes provided inspiration for stories. A visit to a divided Berlin in 1986, which included meetings on both sides of the Wall, led to a story entitled, "A Berlin of the Mind," based on the geography of the place projected into western psychology. That story won an Emerging Writer prize from *Passages North* and was reprinted in my collection, *Unreal City* (Wordcraft of Oregon, 1996) and anthologized elsewhere. A 1991 return visit gave another story, "Beyond the Wall," which won no prizes. In 1985, an evening in Utretcht where our conference hosts had arranged a reception in the amazing Museum of Mechanical Musical Instruments there inspired "Gasparini's Organ," reprinted a number of times and also included in *Unreal City.* In 1986, on my way from my mother's funeral in New York to a conference in Helsinki, I spent an involuntary evening in Turku, grounded by an airlines strike; the snow falling on the Apu River inspired a poem that took runner up status in a *Passages North* contest. An evening in Madrid witnessing the debut of five young bullfighters in 1987—the blood was horrible! – gave me "Sally at the Bullfights," also reprinted a few times and translated and short-listed for the Pushcart Prize, as was "Young Lions Across the Water," which came of my business trip to South Africa in 1996. A few days in Venice gave two stories with nearly the same title—a realistic and a surrealistic one—"St Catherine's Foot" and "The Foot of St Catherine," and I slipped away from a meeting in Dublin once to travel up to Mulingar to meet J P Donleavy, which provided an oft-reprinted interview. Translation assignments for the Torture Rehabilitation Center in Copenhagen rendered me privy to information so horrible it had to be purged by fiction – two stories, both short-listed for the Pushcart and later expanded to the novel Greene's Summer (2004). In 1995, each of two short-shorts inspired respectively by trips to Naples, where my baggage was lost, and to Madrid, won the short-story competition of *The European Magazine*, twice in a row.

What I particularly value about the stories that came from my travels is that they gave me something concrete of those trips, a unique souvenir, served as a kind of aide-memoire of my experience of the place. Unfortunately, though, too much of those many early years of travel were really just a blur of airports, taxis and conference and hotel rooms. And when I came to realize that, I decided that I would never again take a trip without researching where I was going. In advance, I would buy a map, guide-books, would familiarize myself with some of the writers and history of the place where I was headed, would arrive a day or two early and prepare an itinerary through which I might make some discovery about the city beyond the walls and runways of its airport or my hotel room or the cramped quarters of a taxi cab speeding along the quickest route to and from the airport or the incidental sights a host might arrange for me to glimpse.

Francis Bacon said, "Writing maketh a precise man." And I began to seek precision, systematically to write about my travels, and to collaborate with Walter Cummins, himself an avid traveler, on this on-line column and later book, *The Literary Explorer* (Del Sol Press, 2005), which includes essays on, to date, nearly forty of the cities we have visited with open eyes and ready notebooks. I have never regretted doing that. For every place I visit, when I research it first and force myself afterwards to write an account of what I have seen there, what I have done, what I have discovered and thought, that place becomes imprinted in my memory, in my experience. I come to know the place in a way I would never do, never did when I merely passively roamed and let its impressions touch me as they would, unaware and unconscious.

I still regret the opportunities I lost through laziness. But I've never regretted those I seized.

MOORED AT STOCKHOLM
The Lamentations of Barbara Hutton

Walter Cummins

THE CONTRAST WAS STARTLING. That morning we had left a spacious six-room apartment in Copenhagen and, after a short flight, mid afternoon unlocked the door to a tiny cabin in a yacht hotel—the Malardrottningen—anchored off Riddarholmen Island, one of the many that make up the city of Stockholm. The bunks far too narrow for a couple, Alison—much more agile than I—volunteered to take the top, and because we couldn't find a ladder, tested it by climbing onto the desk and pulling herself up. Stretched out, she found her nose just inches from the metal ceiling, relieved not to suffer claustrophobia.

A woman at the desk did fetch us a ladder, and it wasn't for several days that we discovered another, slid under the lower bunk, mine. Now we had two. For a few hours one afternoon, our toilet—along with all the others on the ship—stopped functioning. But otherwise it was a perfectly serviceable room if you spent most of your time away exploring the city. In fact, it served as an incentive to be out and about, and we're thankful for that.

Of course, if we had been staying on that yacht many decades ago, when it was a plaything of heiress Barbara Hutton, those 60 hotel cabins would have been just seven suites, overwhelming us with space. But then there's no chance we ever would have been invited as guests in the Hutton social circle. So bunking in the Malardrottningen to enjoy Stockholm was the best we could have hoped for and, in many ways, beyond our expectations.

Despite its limited dimensions, the cabin offered certain charms, mainly the view out the porthole of an expanse of rippling water, granite cliffs, handsome buildings, and, if you craned your neck, the famous Stockholm City Hall off to the right. Being able to walk down a gangplank onto Riddarholmen also satisfied.

The small island offered a wide esplanade at the water's edge, the metal tables around a kiosk that served food and drink, and several important structures—17th century palaces, a church where kings and royals are buried, the Swedish supreme court, and an ancient tower, along with a statue of Birger Jarl, the city's 13th century founder.

Riddarholmen

A short walk on the island's cobblestones and across a bridge over a highway led to Gamla Stan, the old city, the original island of Stockholm's birth, site of the Royal Palace, the Nobel Museum, structures that go back to the 1200s, a network of charming narrow streets and alleys, endless souvenir shops, and thousands of tourists wandering up and down, we among them. Each night after an alfresco dinner, we had the luxury of leaving the bustle to return to the quiet of Riddarholmen and the Malardrottningen, where the only sound was the water lapping against the ship.

Gamla Stan

As far as I know, Barbara Hutton never got to Stockholm on her yacht or anyone else's, never enjoyed this beautiful city of fourteen islands. She seemed to gravitate toward places that offered abundant sun and warmth, like Venice and Marrakech. And she probably wouldn't have liked Sweden. We know she hated Denmark, a country further south. One of her many husbands, Count Haugwitz-Reventlow, father of Lance, her only child, was a Danish aristocrat with an ancestral home. According to C. David Heymann, author of *Poor Little Rich Girl*, "she detested the stark, lonely island of Lolland with its one small village of Saxkobing and its damp and misty climate."

But the owners of the Malardrottningen flaunt its connection with Hutton, naming the ship after her and displaying her photo in public places like the TV lounge and the breakfast dining area, a large portrait on a wall next to the set broadcasting perpetual CNN, pictures of her with several husbands—Cary Grant, Porfirio Rubirosa, Reventlow—one of her beside the count holding her infant son, later a spoiled young man who wrecked sports cars until he was killed in a plane crash at 36, deepening his mother's decline into decadence. But that came later. In these photos, Barbara posed amidst elegance, arm in arm with a handsome man, trying to look happy. A thin, almost gaunt woman, she never pulls it off, even when smiling, though that impression may be biased by what we know about her life.

Barbara Hutton might seem inappropriate as the subject for a literary traveler; but she does have multiple associations with literature. First of all, in her youth she read widely and wrote poems, publishing two books, her first volume, *The Enchanted*, in 1934, when she was 22. That publication probably resulted from her celebrity status and, possibly, a monetary subvention. Heymann, reports that "in Cannes as a teenager, when not playing croquet, Barbara read, tearing through Zola, Flaubert, and Guy de Maupassant." In his autobiography Cary Grant said of their brief marriage that "I remain deeply obliged to her for a welcome education in the beauties of the arts and other evidences of man's capability for gracious expression and graceful living." At her home in Marrakech, she hosted parties and hobnobbed with the likes of Paul and Jane Bowles, Gore Vidal, Andre Gide, Truman Capote, and Tennessee Williams, picking up the tab for elegant soirees of wit and dandyism. William Burroughs was in Tangiers at the same time as Hutton, and the *Burroughs Report* describes Barbara wearing a diadem and sitting "on a sort of throne when she received guests in her whitewashed, crenellated palace in the medina."

For all her poems, reading, and playing hostess to famous writers,

Hutton, at best, hovers on the fringe of a literature, more the subject of gossip columns and potboilers, including a bio-epic movie. In this sense, she fills the role of an archetype, the woman who has more than every material possession, yet leads a life of failure and misery—Christina Onassis. Princess Stephanie, Doris Duke, Barbara's acquaintance and doppelgänger. Today Hutton might have followed the Paris Hilton path, blatant for the masses rather than attempting to inflate great wealth with aristocratic pretensions.

Still in her teens, she owned a 26-room Fifth Avenue duplex, putting our Copenhagen apartment to shame and making our Malardrottningen cabin feel even more cramped. Yet, ironically, for all the space she possessed, including this yacht, she lived confined in a psychic prison. Having everything, she had nothing, desperate in her seeking—her sexual predations, her marriages and affairs, her jewels, her ostentation, her dissipation.

Her debut, according to Heymann, was celebrated in three stages: first, 500 guests at the Fifth Avenue triplex of her uncle Edward and Marjorie Hutton; second, another 500 dining and dancing at Central Park Casino; third, a ball for 1000 at Ritz-Carlton at a cost of $60,000 (when that meant real money) for four orchestras, 200 waiters, 2,000 bottles of champagne, 10,000 roses, and a seven-course midnight supper. Maurice Chevalier as Santa handed out party favors of small gold jewelry cases containing unmounted gems. Rudy Vallee sang. What could life do for an encore?

This extravagant indulgence was inadequate compensation for the unhappiness of her childhood—an unstable mother, maddened by her husband's philandering, who committed suicide when Barbara was four, a ne'er do well father, a catatonic grandmother, and a beloved grandfather, the source of her wealth, who died when Barbara was young. Her inheritance, the millions and millions that made her famous, came from that grandfather, Frank Winfield Woolworth, who founded the chain of dime stores and made a fortune. Her father's family, the Huttons, were also people of wealth, Uncle Edward, the E.F. Hutton who founded the brokerage that once advertised, "When E.

F. Hutton talks, people listen." Today, Woolworth's is liquidated, and E.F. Hutton disintegrated after accusations of mail fraud and money laundering.

Being a young, spoiled, and profligate heiress during the Depression made Barbara both a figure of gossip-column fascination and an object of derision. She was the unnamed subject of the song "I found a million-dollar baby in a five and ten cent store." When Woolworth's workers went on strike, the press mocked her luxuries. Barbara tried to redeem her reputation through contributions to charity in the thirties and during World War Two. Some of her deeds received attention; but it was difficult to overcome such an iconic reputation. If a Barbara Hutton hadn't existed, she probably would have had to be invented.

I've tried to learn the history of the yacht that became the Malardrottningen with no clear results. One source claims that Hutton received the yacht as a gift on her 18th birthday. But if so, why did she in 1936-37, at 24, spend $250,000 for a 157-foot yacht called the Troubadour that was renamed the S.S. Barbara? That ship had nine baths, two elevators, and was berthed at the Lido near Venice. It may have been the ship some writers say she donated for the U.S. war effort, converted to a patrol vessel and used to escort naval conveys.

But some histories of that yacht give conflicting information. A man named Don W. Farrant in an online journal of his World War Two adventures, including overseas voyages on the ship, says it was called the Viking and purchased by the Navy—not donated by Hutton—then renamed the USS St. Augustine. He repeats a tale that "on her shakedown cruise the executive officer was about to retire one night when he noticed a strange switch, or button, on the side of his bunk. He pressed it, and the bulkhead (wall) immediately slid open and his bunk was right next to the bunk of the captain, in the next stateroom!" Although Farrant's trips had gone without incident, he later learned that the St. Augustine had been rammed by an oil tanker off the New Jersey coast, sinking in five minutes and taking down 115 men.

Because the Malardrottningen is nearly 80 feet longer and has no elevator, it can in no way be that ship, even if it had been salvaged from the bottom of the sea. Travel writer Arthur Frommer says, speaking of the Malardrottningen, "During its heyday, this was the most famous motor yacht in the world, the subject of gossip columns everywhere, thanks to the complicated friendships that developed among the passengers and, in some cases, the crew. Built in 1924 by millionaire C. K. G. Billings, it was the largest motor yacht in the world (72m/236 ft.), and was later acquired by the Woolworth heiress, Barbara Hutton." He doesn't say when she bought it, but notes the hotel conversion took place in the early 1980s, just after Hutton died in 1979. Another writer gives the yacht a name and claims, "While Hutton only owned 'Vanadis' for a short time, her name has stuck to the ship like glue and currently provides curiosity and cachet for the present owners who have turned it into a very different hotel." Yet another says the Vanadis was the yacht given to the government during the war and then converted to a hotel. Confusing. Hutton's will contains no mention of a yacht, so the source of our minuscule cabin probably had passed into other hands by the time of her death.

The Malardrottningen

A sad and awful death it was. At 67, she looked much older, traumatized by her son's crash, ravaged by illness, anorexia, and the abuse of alcohol, drugs, and pain killers, desperate for good-looking young gigolos, often oblivious in drunken stupors and blackouts. But by then most of her money was gone, wasted and misappropriated by a dishonest financial manager, greedy studs, her own obsessive spending, shady merchants, and anyone else who could bleed her.

Most people today probably haven't heard of Barbara Hutton. Beyond her bleak biography, she left no real legacy. How long will her name on a yacht-hotel in Stockholm mean anything to travelers? Other more recent desolate lives have become more memorable, more in tune with our time, when profligacy is commonplace and a story like Barbara's almost a cliché.

Yet here's one of her youthful poems, "Expectation," not quite literature, more a commentary on her relationship to the world:

> I must sing a song of ecstasy,
> They expect it of me;
> And I must laugh
> To fill the world with glee,
> They expect it of me.
>
> A thousand joyous things
> I must do,
> They expect me to.
>
> Well, the devil take them
> And their expectations,
> All they will get from me
> Is lamentations.

Would it have made a difference if she had gone through life as a cabin passenger, experiencing the hard knocks of an upper berth, finding joy in a view of Stockholm?

SHOOT TO MAIM—SMILE TO DISARM
A Visit to Two Danish Prisons

Thomas E. Kennedy

Recently, an American friend, Dave Sorensen, an associate professor of criminology at the University of Copenhagen, invited me to join class visits to two categories of Danish prison—the open prison at Jyderup in western Zealand and the maximum security prison, Vridsløselille State Prison, in Albertslund—respectively about an hour and a half by bus and 25 minutes by city train from central Copenhagen.

Dave Sorensen and Thomas E. Kennedy

I've read various books about people who are imprisoned, both fiction and nonfiction—Camus' *The Stranger*, Dostoyevsky's *The House of the Dead* and *Crime and Punishment*, and more recently Tom Wolfe's *A Man in Full* and a nonfiction book, *The Hot House: Life Inside Leavenworth Prison* by Pete Earley. I've also had friends who were draft dodgers in the 1960s, were captured and served time and came out looking different—pale, hard, hurt. In more recent years, the subject of rape and sexual slavery in prison have come to the surface and become so much a part of popular folklore that, to an American, imprisonment is almost synonymous with the likelihood of anal rape: Either you're a man or a punk. And to avoid being made into a punk you have to do something to prove your brutality—like sticking a toothpick in your tormenter's eyeball. Tom Wolfe describes that sexual fear powerfully in his 1998 novel, *A Man in Full*, in which an ordinary citizen, through a series of mischances, winds up in jail and is selected by the tough guy leader of an enclave of white neo-Nazi prisoners as his next punk. Wolfe—who is perhaps a better researcher and reporter than novelist—also portrays the character of an American prison in a vivid and seemingly genuine manner:

The Old Barracks at Santa Rita were built like barns, with big, gloomy, dark wooden bays two stories high. The cells were unlike any jail cells Conrad had ever heard of. They were stalls, or perhaps the word was sties, since as on many pig farms, they were made of dirty beige concrete and plaster. Each cell was about 5 by 9 feet, barely big enough for a double decker metal bunk, bolted to the floor, and a unit-welded metal toilet-and-basin ensemble. There were no windows, and the door was a solid slab of wood like a ship's hatch, painted black with a slot for passing in food. Instead of a ceiling, each cell had a heavy wire screen for a cover.... When you looked up through the screen you saw the underside of a wooden cat-walk where the deputies patrolled, peering down at the creatures below. Somewhere above the catwalks were windows for light and air. A few ancient, belt-driven attic fans were always grinding and screeching away, but the heat kept pressing down. It never lifted, not even at night.

Dostoyevsky, in *The House of the Dead* (1860), a nonfiction account of his ten years in a Siberian prison, painted a picture no brighter:

> Our prison stood at the edge of the fortress, right next to the ramparts. You would sometimes take a look at God's world through the cracks in the fence....and all you would see would be a corner of sky and the high earthen ramparts, overgrown with weeds, and on

> the ramparts, the sentries pacing up and down, day and night; and then you would think that whole years would go by, and you would still come to look through the cracks in the fence and would see the same ramparts, the same sentries, and the same little corner of the sky, not the sky that stood above the prison, but another, distant and free.... When it got dark we were all taken back to the barracks, where we were locked up for the whole night. I always found it hard to come into our barrack from outside. It was a long, low unventilated room, dimly lit...with a heavy suffocating smell. I do not understand now how I managed to live in it for ten years.

I read Dostoyevsky's book when I was 17, Wolfe's when I was in my 50s. For those decades I've been convinced that all prisons are like that—or worse. But my recent visits to two Danish prisons have given me cause to believe that things here in Denmark—and potentially elsewhere—might be different, might include a possibility for humane treatment, even rehabilitation. Winston Churchill—who had himself been a POW in the Boer War—once said that you can judge a country on the way it treats its prisoners.

Denmark's prison system includes approximately 14 open prisons and 4 or 5 maximum security prisons. Some complain that going to prison in Denmark is like a state-paid hotel stay. I found this not to be the case. Clearly it is not pleasant to be in prison in Denmark either—you are deprived of your freedom. That is your punishment. You are locked in. Or you are within view of an open gate which you may not walk through. The Danish penal system is a humane one with considerable freedom of movement.

The inmates purchase and prepare their own food (and knives are freely available in the kitchen—which have not been used for violent ends). The inmates wash their own clothes, have access to a gym and walk about freely on the grounds which are green and fenced in, though not locked off. My group was shown around by a woman guard (unarmed) and a long-term prisoner who was soon to be released after many years in prison and would assume work as a blacksmith, which trade he had learned in prison.

Our prisoner guide told me that he spent the first part of his sentence in a maximum security facility where the guards were armed and conditions evoked violent emotions in him which he had to fight to control. In the open facility, clearly the guard and prisoner were on easy terms, talked and joked with one another. He said that his incentive to behave was that if he did not behave, he risked being sent back to the maximum security facility. There was a possibility to work and take education, to be accompanied on visits to the local town, order books from the public library. Although the inmates were not allowed to have cell phones (a new rule, imposed politically from above), they were allowed to have telephones in their rooms and to call out.

The advantage is that the system offers a hand up to people who have had trouble adjusting to society rather than to brutalize them further and make them even more unfit for society. It was impressively humane —but not like a hotel. The loss of freedom was apparent. I felt claustrophobic visiting the rooms—and the isolation facility even more so. The inmates are locked into their rooms from 9.00 p.m. to 7.00 a.m. because those are the hours—in prison and outside—during which violence is more likely to occur—the hour of the wolf as Ingmar Bergman described it in his film of that title.

Another major cause of violence in prison is the deprivation of sexual communion with another human being. In a Danish open prison, the inmate's wife or partner (whether hetero or homo) and children are free to visit on weekends and to have privacy in the inmate's room. Prisoners who don't have a partner may have a visit from a prostitute (prostitution is legal here, though profiting off of prostitutes is not). I cannot refrain from comparing this to a report I had recently from a friend whose daughter was arrested for DUI. When her mother visited her there was a plexi-glass sheet between them—they could not touch. When the mother attended her court hearing, she asked the court guard if she might be allowed to give her little girl (she was 20) a hug; the uniformed officer said, "Honey, not only can't you hug her, you're not allowed to make eye contact with her either!"

My criminology professor friend, Dave Sorensen, has surveyed prison systems in many other countries and was optimistic about the system here. In the end, recividism results are difficult to compare; in the American system many more elderly men are discharged from prison, having been away for very long sentences and less likely, at that age, to be equipped to commit crimes. In the Danish system, however, the maximum sentence is 12 years, in very exceptional cases 16, and parole is possible much earlier. Those who complain about the good treatment of prisoners here seem to me stuck in the Old Testament idea of justice—eye for eye, tooth for tooth, sin and you shall suffer. And how odd that neo-con Christians should ignore the humanity which distinguishes Christ.

At the end of our tour, the 25 of us were invited into the prison lunch room for a Q&A session with the woman guard and the prisoner who had shown us around. The prisoner spoke freely about the conditions he had experienced in both maximum security and open prison in Denmark. He blamed the atmosphere in the closed prison for getting him into trouble which had extended his sentence. He had been locked in for 12 years. He told about the availability of drugs in prison and how he, himself, had been a dealer in the beginning—how he had even been selling drugs to people in the local town. And he told how prisoners in the maximum security prisons

Touring Students

did not speak with the guards—to do so would entail a loss of honor in the eyes of the other prisoners.

So, it seemed to me, there is still a counterpart in Denmark of the inhumane atmosphere of the American prison—despite the fact that the woman guard who had shown us around looked teasingly at him and said, "Have you taken your medication today?" At which the prisoner, with a self-ironic smile, said, "I think I forgot." And sotto voce muttered, "They're going to start making me take them again."

This left me with a question mark. Our visit to the maximum security prison was still two weeks off, and I wondered what might be in store for us there—in a climate where prisoners and guards speak with one another only out of necessity, where—I got the impression—guards are armed and prisoners aggressive, offenders of the worst sort.

Perhaps this would require the sort of prison described in Pete Earley's *The Hot House: Life inside Leavenworth Prison* (1992):

> Six gun towers protect [Leavenworth Prison], and each employee, including clerical workers, prison counselors, and even the prison psychologist, is expected to spend time in them at some point during his or her career.... When people apply for a job at Leavenworth, they are asked what they would do if they saw an inmate climbing the wall. The correct answer is 'shoot to maim.' Anyone who says they are not willing to shoot an inmate is not hired.

That description would seem to indicate that, in the century and a half since the prison described in Dostoyevsky's *The House of the Dead*, conditions in an American prison had not become much better than conditions in a Russian one—in some manner perhaps even worse.

The next visit, again led by Associate Professor Dave Sorensen, was to the maximum security prison with the tongue-twisting name of Vridsløselille, 25 minutes by city train southwest of central Copenhagen, a five-minute walk from the Albertslund station.

The state prison at Vridsløselille began operation in 1859—a year before the publication of Dostoyevsky's nonfiction book. Unlike the Jyderup facility, this structure looks like a prison with a massive double-turreted front wall and a broad solid barn-door port. This façade is well-known to the audience of popular Danish film, from a series of 1970s Danish comedies about the Olsen Gang, three bumbling thieves. Each film in the series begins with the Olsen Gang's mastermind, Egon Olsen, being released from this massive prison port, and each film concludes with him being locked into it again, after his latest convoluted plan to crack a safe has failed. The actor who played Egon Olsen in the half dozen or so films died recently, and was honored by having the road leading up to the prison doors named after him: Egon Olsens Way.

Vridsløselille Prison in Albertslund

I can feel the butterflies in my stomach at the thought of being led through a gamut of violent prisoners who might snarl at us, make provocative comments. I remember our prison inmate tour guide from Jyderup and wonder—was he merely off his medications or was he revealing the truth beneath the glossy surface of the Danish system.

Our group of ten is met outside the gate by an Assistant Warden named "Marianne," a woman in her late 30s, dressed in casual clothes. She carries no weapon and has no emergency alarm device on her belt. Her only visible weapon is a disarmingly shy smile. She admits us through the port where a secretary named Lone collects our cell phones in a plastic shopping bag and gives them to a desk guard locked behind a window. This is a new rule, imposed by the increasingly conservative Danish politicians who feel it is too comfortable for prisoners to be allowed to have cell phones or personal computers. They may write to whomever they wish, however, and their mail may only be inspected in cases of grounded suspicion and following specific procedures, may use the public phones in their wards, and may rent private TVs for their cells.

Minus our cell-phones—though without passing through a metal detector or any other manner of security search, we are let through an antique, barred, wrought-iron gate which locks behind us with a clang as we enter the prison itself.

The prison was originally built in the classic panopticon form—the word panopticon was used by the English philosopher of law Jeremy Bentham (1748-1832) to describe a model prison, constructed such that the positioning of the guards in a central watchtower allowed them to see all the cells from one single viewpoint. According to the Ministry of Justice description, this was originally a cellular confinement prison (so-called Philadelphia Prison), where the inmates were segregated during work and in their leisure time. The prison is star-shaped with four three-storied wings, emanating from a central building ("the center") with place for 249 prisoners.

The secretary Lone tells us that during her 28 years working here, the central watchtower was taken down and walls were built up so that instead of cells, the prison is divided into closed sections with private rooms.

We climb the stairs and are admitted to one of the "sections"—each of which houses about twenty prisoners. The prisoners are currently at work or school, which they attend from 9:00 to 3:00 each weekday. When they return from work at 3.00, they are locked into their section but are free to circulate there with the others or to go into their rooms. The section consists of a central passage which is perhaps 50 meters long and 6 meters wide with a ping-pong table in the middle. There is a security station to the right inside the door where a uniformed, though unarmed guard sits, and the walls to left and right are lined with windowless doors that lead to the cells (more like rooms, each perhaps 3 meters wide and 5 or 6 deep, containing a bed, writing desk, water closet and—in the cell I saw—small refrigerator and TV. Although there is no window in the door, there is one in the far wall, a large window behind screened bars. The room is small. I've stayed in hotel rooms this small, though rarely, and a major difference is that the hotel-room door opened from the inside. Once, in a hotel on the Grand Place in Brussels, when offered a room this small with no window, I immediately broke into a sweat and demanded another. In these rooms, the prisoners are locked from 9.00 p.m. until 7.00 a.m.—8.00 a.m. on weekends.

There are people who complain that such "soft," non-punishing treatment does not entail any crime deterrent, that these criminals—thieves, robbers, drug dealers, men convicted of violent crimes, murderers—are simply sent away to a hotel to serve out their time. But the philosophy of the Danish penal system is that the punishment is the loss of liberty and that that is sufficient punishment, while attempting to prepare the prisoners for readmission to a non-criminal life when they have completed their sentences. Contemplating 10 or 11 hours locked in that tiny room every night, I have to agree—it is sufficient punishment. But it is not excessive. It is not retribution or retaliation. It is corrective confinement, in the true sense of the term.

Our group gathers in the kitchen—at the center of the one side wall. As in the open prison, the inmates wash their own clothes, clean their own area, shop for their own food and, in groups of three or four, make their own meals. The kitchen is large enough that the 10 of us and our 2 guides can range comfortably around the walls. In the center is a kind of square table stove, perhaps a meter long on each side with two hot plates per side. Mounted on the wall are a row of carving knives which catch our attention.

The knives are not locked away. There are violent men here, murderers. As an American, says one of the students, this strikes me as insane. Has there ever been a violent crime committed here with one of those knives? Lone, the secretary, a relaxed woman in her late 50s perhaps, wearing jeans and a T-shirt, tells us that in her 28 years here there has been a single incident in which one prisoner slit another's throat with a kitchen knife, but only that once, and there has never been violence against a guard. What if one of the prisoners steals a knife? Then all the rooms would be searched thoroughly. But they won't do that because they know that then they risk having the knives locked up, and it is much nicer to have a kitchen where you can use a knife without having to ask a guard to unlock it for you and watch over you when you use it. Makes sense to me.

Lone lifts the shirt jacket of Marianne to show she is wearing no emergency alarm device. "It's a matter of mutual trust," she says. "I work up in my section there, and one day last week, for example, there were eight inmates who were..." She makes quotation marks with her fingers. "...sick so they didn't go to work. They stayed in their section all day playing pool. One of them looked at me and said, 'You don't wear an alarm?' It's a matter of trust. In 28 years, nothing has ever happened to me here. We also joke with each other, the inmates and the personnel. Not from the start. If you try teasing a guy who is new here, he might misunderstand. But later, they relax." She tells us how a year ago, just before Christmas, they moved in on some of the inmates who they'd discovered were making liquor. They were fermenting rye bread and the smell was very strong and gave it away. She tells how the inmates asked why they waited until right before Christmas. "That way you didn't have time to make more for Christmas," she explained.

Is it a problem that so many of the guards are women? "Only when it is time for a strip search," says Lone. "Only a male guard here may strip search a male prisoner. In Sweden, the women guards do it, too—just as in the hospitals, it is not required to have a male nurse for male patients. But it is not allowed here." She shrugs.

The inmates have frequent visits and nuptial visits (up to 7 hours a week) and, after a while in prison, are allowed to go home to visit their families. The aim is always to keep from institutionalizing the inmate, to do all that can be done to keep him fit for re-entry to society as a law-abiding citizen. As reported after the visit to Jyderup Open Prison, the philosophy here is the same—that the inmates are allowed to continue their sexual life with a wife, partner of either gender, or a prostitute. The prime cause of prison violence is considered to be a result of sexual deprivation; thus, the violence in Danish prisons is drastically less frequent, perhaps almost non-existent.

In the open prison we were told that prisoners convicted of sexual offenses were not popular. The other prisoners might say to them, "Ask for a transfer. We don't want you here." There have been beatings, too, but with fists, not debilitating attacks or murders.

One of the students asks what the inmates would do with a cell phone if they were allowed to have one Was there a danger of the prisoners using a cellphone to mastermind an escape or engage in further crime? . Lone replies by kissing up her lips. "They say they just want to be able to phone the little woman and kiss her goodnight." This gives a new insight: Picture a man locked into his tiny room for 10 or 11 hours every night, thinking about his woman—"Oh, my love, my darling, I hunger for your touch/The long, lonely nights..." Why not?

We also visit one of the 12-step sections (a so-called "contract unit"), to which inmates are admitted voluntarily to undergo a so-called Minnesota cure—the 12-step program which helps people out of alcohol and/or drug addiction. When admitted to this program, a prisoner has to sign a paper which commits him to remain for as long as it takes him, even if his prison term is shorter than required for the cure. We are greeted in the otherwise empty section by an inmate of 30 or so, tall and good-looking, wearing shorts, tee shirt and sandals. He has agreed to field our questions. Because we are an international group the session is conducted in English, and he apologizes that he has only gone to school up to grade 9 and that his English is not very good. We assure him it is excellent, and he tells how he has learned not to be so aggressive and full of fear and lacking in humility. He explains how the program helps you to learn fellowship and humility, to think positively and constructively. He is currently in step four of the program and he longs for the day when he will get home to his wife and two children.

My heart goes out to this young man. He longs for what every man longs for—to be home with his family, to be worthy of respect, to have a job. His uncertainty and sorrow show beneath the surface of his face as does his wish to transcend and earn back his right to a good life. It seems to me a good system that gives its inmates that kind of hope and possibility.

We are led out through the prison yard that is reserved for the drug rehab section. Because of the danger of drugs being present in the prison, the 12-steppers are isolated from the other prisoners and are given frequent urine tests to ensure that they are drug-free. If drug traces are found in their urine, they are immediately ejected from the program, out into the general population. Through another gate we go out into the common prison yard—broad and grassy, enclosed by tall yellow-brick walls. It was one of those walls which, about ten years before, was suddenly smashed down from the outside by a huge truck, allowing ten prisoners to make a run for it. In some mysterious way, a TV crew had been on hand and filmed the whole event. All the escapees were re-arrested, most within a very short time. Assistant Warden Marianne smiles at the thought of it, and I cannot help but contrast her disarming smile with the requirement placed upon Leavenworth personnel, who are not hired unless they assert their willingness to shoot a prisoner trying to escape. Shoot to maim. This is an utterly different world.

The last stop on our tour is the prison chapel. To get there we have to pass once again through the central hub of the prison complex, and as we are about to leave one section, we run into a group of inmates returning to their section from the gym. Here there is a metal detector, but not for us; the prisoners have to pass through it. Marianne apologizes to them as we back up to the walls of the corridor so the inmates can pass through. I see a range of expressions on their faces—from annoyance to blankness to disdain to cheerful curiosity. One of them smiles, waving his hand to either side, saying, "Hello hello." We return his greeting, and the last of them passes through the screener.

Marianne leads us now into the chapel. The rear wall is a high-pitched window that looks out to the grass and the sky, though massive yellow brick walls are also visible. Beside the altar is a drum kit, and three electric guitars hang on the wall. The prison band—Prison Choir—also plays here and has made a couple of gospel CDs. On the altar is a small reproduction of Thorvaldsen's magnificent marble Jesus, the original of which stands in Our Lady Cathedral in Copenhagen. Thorvaldsen's Jesus is not a bleeding, crucified martyr, but a strong, healthy man with a powerful body, a man of action, his arms open to embrace humanity.

The man who is waiting for us in the chapel, named Povl, seated on the altar steps, also has a powerful body, thick arms and a broad deep chest and sloping shoulders. He is the inmate spokesman and sports director, Macedonian of origin. He has served eight of his 10½ year sentence and admits to us, answering a question from one of the students, that he worries whether he will be able to take care of his wife and children when he finally gets out. For his final years in prison he will apply to serve out his time in an open prison where he hopes that he will be able to learn the trade of a plumber.

Somehow he inspires more daring questions. One student asks about racial friction in the prison. We are told that about 30% of the inmate population is non-Danish but that the friction is no greater than on the outside. What about gangs? Povl explains that there is only one gang here—the Bandidos motorcycle gang—but its members are isolated in their own segment of the prison, as the Hells Angels—their rival gang—are isolated in a special section of another prison. This is the Danish way of ensuring that the gangs do not take over and enslave the other prisoners.

Someone asks Povl whether he thinks it is a good place here.

"Of course," he says, "I wish I was free. But since I have to be in prison, I think this is a good place. I saw a program on the television—think it is called Discovery Channel—about American prisons.

They also have open prisons there, but the maximum security prisons—they are like cages for wild animals. You know," he says, "I don't think that is a good idea."

He considers for a moment, his mouth serious, then looks at us in a significant way. "Let me ask you," he says. "If you put a dog into a miserable cage like that and keep it locked away there for years, and then you come to let him out again, what do you think the dog will do? Don't you think he would attack you?"

Those interested in more information can consult the website of the Danish Ministry of Justice and the following publications: *A Programme of Principles for Prison and Probation Work in Denmark; and Danish Prison and Probation Service.*

Photographs by Charlotte Chinnery

"NO REAL REASON FOR A TOURIST TO STOP" Buonconvento, Tuscany

Walter Cummins

Ideal villages have a tendency to morph into tourist destinations, the picturesque structures where people lived and worked for centuries converted into restaurants and souvenir shops, hordes of day visitors wandering up and down narrow lanes licking cones of glace or gelato. I'm thinking of Aigues Morte in the French Camargue, Les Baux in Provence, Riquewihr in Alsace, San Gigmignano and Pienza in Tuscany. Pienza, in particular, is perfectly preserved, in fact was designed to be perfect by a fifteenth-century Pope named Pius II, who collaborated with an architect, Bernardo Gambarelli, to transform the small village of his birth into a papal residence of grace and balance high in the Tuscan hills. Franco Zeffirelli used it to substitute for Verona in his 1968 version of *Romeo and Juliet*. When we visited in the mid nineties, gesturing men pointed our Peugeot toward a field off to the side of the village, where long rows of daytrip cars lined the grass. After paying the parking fee, we joined the people strolling the streets, admiring piazzas and palaces and enjoying a fine meal in an elegant restaurant.

At the time we were spending several weeks in a converted fifteenth-century stone tobacco barn on a farm just minutes outside a town called Buonconvento located on the SS2 highway twelve miles south of Siena, not far from the road that circled up the hillside to Montalcino, where Brunello wines come from. The concept behind our stay is called agriturismo, farmers refurbish-

ing outbuildings as accommodations for short-term visitors.

Buonconvento doesn't attract many visitors beyond the Germans driving through, their Audi trunks loaded with cases of wine. It's a place where locals shop for staples in a tiny Coop, fresh bread in a bakery, fresh produce at a vegetable stand. We were among the first English speakers to spend time in the region, I rising early in a quest for one of the few *Herald Tribune*s at the village newsstand, the man behind the counter frowning with a thumbs down "finito" when I came too late, brightening with an exuberant "Yes!" the rare days a copy was left

The Main Street, da Mario in the Middle

We ate a number of meals in a small restaurant called Da Mario, run by a mother, grandmother, and son, all with the same face in various stages of age and gender. As much as she smiled at the diners, the mother scolded the hangdog son, who seemed unable to do anything right. The grandmother stirred steaming pots in the tiny kitchen, the mother took orders, and the son made mistakes. None spoke English, but that was true of the whole town. The mother did know enough to say, "We gots spaghetti, ravioli, lasagna." That was the primi course. Some form of carne appeared in the segundi, though primi was usually filling for us. Bottles of local wine sat on every table, washed and refilled daily, stopped with corks you could pull out with your fingers. The price of the wine seemed to change from day to day, sometimes 2,000 lire, sometimes 2,500. At the pre-euro exchange rate that was about a dollar fifty to a dollar seventy-five. The wine was drinkable. Sort of.

Much of the time we were content to stay on the farm, watching the grazing sheep on the hillside, the vineyards and olive groves, the wheat fields turning from green to golden. There were paths for long walks, clean air to breathe, miles of the Tuscan hills to gaze at, after dark the lights of distant villages. We could take in the whole of Buonconvento slightly below our vantage point, on some evenings feel the throbbing rhythms that rose from the local discothèque.

Though Buonconvento was comprised of only a handful of blocks, I never tired of walking among then, seeing the towering entrance and massive wooden gates that were always open, maneuvering through the narrow alleys just behind the main street of shops, where drying laundry hung from almost every window.

Since then I came to hold that memory as somewhat exclusive. I've run into a number of people who told me about their afternoons among the towers of San Gigmignano and other Tuscan must-sees. No one goes to Buonconvento. So I was surprised to open the *New York Times Magazine* one recent Sunday to discover a food report by Maggie Barrett devoted to the town's fall harvest festival.

But Barrett cautions, "Apart from the 10-day sagra (or harvest festival) in September and the one-night festa della prima luna d'estate (the first-moon-of-summer festival) in June . . . there is no real reason for a tourist to stop here." Before offering recipes, the article does make the fall feast enticing:

> How thrilling it is to participate in this community experience. For 10 days the town joins together to celebrate not only the harvest but also the importance of tradition and collaboration. During the day, visitors walk down the streets and alleys and, led by their noses, peer into the many cantinas, where women, from 50 to 90, are rolling out pasta dough, building lasagnas, chopping the tomatoes for crostini. Huge vats of chickpeas simmer on a stove. A gas ring on the floor holds an enormous pot of polenta that is patiently stirred by a great-grandmother. Parboiled potatoes sit in immense pans waiting for lard shavings to accompany them into the oven. Across the alley, trays of jam rolls lie in rows like bambini in a nursery while the women prepare torta di nonna — grandmother's cake.

So it's clear that Buonconvento has its brief lure for gourmets with a certain culinary disposition. But what about literary travelers? Its setting in the midst of the Tuscan landscape amid the light and colors seen in the backgrounds of so many Renaissance paintings and its proximity to Siena and, a bit farther, Florence conjure up a history of artistic masterpieces and Renaissance splendor. Yet what of Buonconvento itself?

It certainly played a role in Dante's fate as part of the tangle of Guelph (supporters of the Pope) and Ghibelline (supporters of the emperor) politics. Dante took the side of a faction called the White

Guelphs, who lost control of Florence to the Black Guelphs when he was on a diplomatic mission to Rome. Exiled from the city in 1302, Dante was counting on Henry VII, Emperor of Luxembourg, to lead a triumphant military campaign that would oust his enemies and allow the poet to return to the city he loved. Here's what one source has to say about Henry:

> An idealist who believed that as God's secular vicar he had a divine mission to restore peace to "the garden of the Empire," Henry entered Italy in 1310 with the consent of Pope Clement V (1305-14) and seemed at first to prosper. He sought, as an honest broker, to reconcile Guelph (i.e., pro-papal) and Ghibelline (i.e., pro-imperial) factions, but it was soon apparent that any attempt to override those old loyalties implied a massive assault upon the political status quo, a revolution that would be fiercely resisted. Florence, in particular, saw as unacceptable not simply any concession to its enemies but any restoration of imperial power..

Henry doesn't seem to have been much of a military strategist, considering his constant indecision and dawdling. On August 24, 1313, he died, probably of a fever, in Buonconvento. One story claims he was poisoned in sacramental bread by a Dominican friar, bribed by the powers in Florence. But that's disputed. Whatever happened to cause Henry's death—murder or natural causes—Dante suffered a grave disappointment, one that affected the course of his life. Buonconvento probably played an accidental role in all this, merely the location of an event that became a footnote in history. Still, when the bad news reached Dante, he may have heard the name Buonconvento and it may have stuck in his memory. He may even have cursed the town, though he didn't have the enmity to condemn it in the *Inferno*.

Coincidentally, Giovanni Boccaccio, a younger Florentine who wrote a brief life of Dante, includes Buonconvento in one of the tales in *The Decameron*, specifically:

> THE NINTH DAY, THE FOURTH NOVELL

> SERVING AS AN ADMONITION TO ALL MEN, FOR TAKING GAMESTERS AND DRUNKARDS INTO THEIR SERVICE
>
> Francesco Fortarigo, played away all that he had at Buonconvento, and likewise the money of Francesco Aniolliero, being his Master. Then running after him in his shirt, and avouching that hee had robbed him: he caused him to be taken by Pezants of the Country, clothed himselfe in his Masters wearing garments, and (mounted on his horse) rode thence to Sienna, leaving Aniolliero in his shirt, and walked barefooted.

Of course, all that happened in the fourteenth century when political treachery abounded, when even emperors died of fever (or poison), when people fled cities to escape the plague, and when servants cheated their masters. In the Buonconvento I knew, the worst that happened was a shortage of *Herald Tribunes*—no baseball scores, no crossword puzzles. Finito.

ANGELS IN DISGUISE: SHAKESPEARE AND CO. A Few Words, a Few Pictures

Thomas E. Kennedy

ENOUGH HAS BEEN WRITTEN about the wonderful Latin-Quarter antiquarian bookshop, Shakespeare And Co., on the left bank of the Seine in Paris, that I feel free to make this brief. But I *must* say a few words about this "wonderland of books," as Henry Miller called it, and share some of my photographs of it.

The original Shakespeare And Co was run by Sylvia Beach from 1919 to 1941 at 12 rue de l'Odeon. There it was that James Joyce's Ulysses was first published, a shop frequented by Hemingway, Fitzgerald, Pound, Ford Maddox Ford, Gertrude Stein, Joyce and others.

Shakespeare And Co. in Winter, Febrary 2005

Around 1950, an American expatriate in Paris named George Whitman—son of Walt (not Walt the Brooklyn poet, but Walt the Massachusetts text-book author)—purchased with the help of a small inheritance a site that had housed an Arab grocer at 37 rue de la Bûcherie in the fifth arrondisement, across the Seine from Notre Dame, and opened a bookstore there that he called *Le Mistral*—after the wind that blows across the Mediterranean from Africa to the south coast of France. Among his clientele and friends were Henry Miller, Graham Greene, Anais Nin, Langston Hughes, James Jones, James Baldwin, William Styron, Richard Wright, Ginsburg, Corso, Ferlinghetti, and many others, including Sylvia Beach. In 1964, after Sylvia Beach had died, Whitman renamed his shop Shakespeare And Co in her honor. Since then, he also named his daughter after her—Sylvia Beach Whitman.

There the shop has been for well over half a century now, weathering legal assaults by the French authorities, book-destroying fires and tiresome lease squabbles, still standing after all those years, as of this writing still run by George and his daughter Sylvia. Ironically, the French authorities who over the years ago had hassled George for not having the papers required of foreign merchants in France have recently awarded him one of France's highest honors—Officier de l'Ordre des Arts et Lettres, a badge on a ribbon with a rosette worn on the left side of the chest.

I discovered this great place only fifteen years ago, in the early 1990s. I had recently published my first novel, *Crossing Borders,* which was as unknown as I. Scheduled to read from it that evening at a now alas defunct literary center called The Foundry, founded by David Applefield and John Calder, I took a walk through the fifth and visited Shakespeare And Co. As I stepped through the door, I saw George Whitman himself seated behind the cash register, reading. I recognized him from photos.

"Excuse me, Mr. Whitman," I began, "my name is Tom Kennedy and..."

He rose. He took my hand. He said, "Tom Kennedy! From Copenhagen! Your bed is all ready for you upstairs. And you must be our guest of honor at our literary tea on Sunday."

How he knew my name or where I came from is a mystery I never solved—perhaps he simply knew every single detail of what was happening in Paris that might be of even the most remote interest to literary-minded people.

Since then I visit the Whitman wonderland whenever I am in Paris, usually several times per visit. I love to browse and hang around, eavesdropping on the conversations around the cash register area—a kind of conversation pit – and up in the second floor reading room, which is equipped not only with books but with lounging beds and a little typewriter niche for the inspired. Mostly young people gather there, and the conversation and faces are rich with the hope and enthusiasm and ideas that continue to make Paris the world capital of literary expatriatism, lost generation after beat generation after hippie generation after whatever generation we may have reached now.

George Whitman and Sylvia Beach Whitman, above the shop, February 2005

Last year on a visit, I had the good fortune of meeting George, now in his 95th year, and his lovely young daughter, Sylvia Beach Whitman, in her early twenties, and they invited me up to the private rooms above the shop. There they sat, surrounded by books, smiling like a couple of generations of angel, clearly devoted to one another and to books and to the shop and its motto: *Be Not Inhospitable to Strangers Lest They Be Angels in Disguise.*

Upstairs

Upstairs: A visitor lounges in the reading room

ROAMING LITERARY LONDON
Bloomsbury and Environs

Walter Cummins

You could devote a lifetime—and some actually have—to roaming London as a literary explorer. Stroll down street after street to discover blue plaques on buildings that proclaim some writer you read in a survey of Brit Lit course lived there for a few years. Or follow the fictional footsteps of Clarissa Dalloway through Westminster on her morning quest for flowers. Or tour the locales of Eliot's Wasteland: "'This music crept by me upon the waters' / And along the Strand, up Queen Victoria Street / O City city, I can sometimes hear / Beside a public bar in Lower Thames Street . . ." And that's not to mention Dickens and Thackeray and Ben Jonson and Samuel Johnson and Evelyn Waugh and Anthony Powell. Is there a London street or park or landmark that hasn't appeared in some novel or poem or play or story over the centuries?

So what is a traveler to do to avoid being overwhelmed? My most recent strategy—other than a tube trip to Southwark to see the reconstruction of Shakespeare's

Globe Theatre—was to stay within walking distance of the flat we had rented in a narrow alley behind the Russell Square tube station. Even with that limitation, I barely touched all the possibilities.

The British Library

The new—opened in 1998—British Library at St. Pancras was just ten minutes away up Woburn Place, with a left turn on Euston Road. The young man in the nearby pub claimed the library was shaped like a ship, the design visible if you looked down from the upper stories of the building next door, a view he had often enjoyed because he was friendly with the concierge. The description on the museum's website is more prosaic: "The plan of the building resembled something akin to an inverted letter A, in technical terms a rhomboid, being shortest to the south (Euston Road) with sides tapering outward towards the longer end approaching Brill Place in the direction of Camden Town."

Construction of the new library became controversial because of cost and sentiment. It took twenty years from the development of the original plans to the day of the Queen's ceremonial opening. During that time a series of builders' delays and price escalations frustrated the project and led to public grousing. Budgetary constraints resulted in a structure only two-thirds the intended size.

Years before when I first heard about the intention of relocating the library from the British Museum to a location that had been "a derelict goods yard immediately to the west of St Pancras station" I was one of the unhappy many. Thousands of serious scholars, including a number of American friends with readers' passes, had conducted research in the museum reading room. They lamented the change of an institution with such personal meaning to them.

While never a scholar, my emotional tie to the museum library struck on my first visit to the manuscript cases, actually seeing the handwriting of authors I had read and even passed examinations on. Jane Austen and Oscar Wilde and Virginia Woolf and so many others. It somehow added a new level of actuality to all those books, the excitement of standing in the midst of an authenticity beyond my imaginings—ascension into English major's heaven.

How could soulless bureaucrats violate that sacred space? They did—eventually—and people in general, the vast majority, are happy with the results, the new British Library serving as one of London's most visited tourist attractions. And the manuscripts are there too, in different display cases, not looked down on from about, but mainly at eye level. Austen, Woolf, and Wilde, Joyce's *Ulysses* too, and so are hand-lettered *Beowulf, Sir Gawain and the Green Knight*, and Thomas Malory's *Le Morte D'Arthur,* works I didn't remember from my earlier visits to the British Museum. It may be that the new displays are actually easier to see.

Beyond literary works, the cases house illuminated manuscripts, Medieval Codices, a Guttenberg Bible, musical scores by Mozart and others, letters from scientists like Charles Babbage and Alfred Russel Wallace, and political figures like Gladstone, Florence Nightingale, original Beatles lyrics on scraps of paper in various childish handwritings (with headphones for listening to their performance), and an entire alcove devoted to the history and drafts of the Magna Carta.

The days I visited, racks displayed entries in a bookbinding contest to recover nominees for the previous year's Man Booker prize, leather of various colors and hand-tooled lettering. For the cover of a book on fish the replica of a fish tail and fish head protruded from the front. A bit over the top, some might say. But the general detail and workmanship celebrated the physical book as an art object on its own.

Visually, the literal centerpiece of the British Library is a six-story wood-framed glass tower holding the complete library of King George III that contains about 65,000 books and 19,000 pamphlets. While that king's sanity is questioned (as in *The Madness of George III*) and the American Colonies were lost during his reign, he did create the foundation of a national British library. There are worse legacies for a ruler.

The collection, of course, has expanded far beyond 65,000. According to the 2006 report, it houses close to 13.5 million books, more than three-quarters of a million serials, more than 8 million philatelic and 4 million cartographic items, 1.5 million musical scores, and many other objects. So what if it's shaped more like a rhomboid than a ship?

The British Museum, by the way, still has a reading room that focuses on books relating to the museum's collections, such as history, art, and travel. It's been situated in the middle of the Great Court since 1857 and still deserves a visit. That too was only a few minutes from our flat in the alley.

Dickens' House

The building at 48 Doughty Street, in a long row of similar structures, was just one of Dickens' London homes, the only one turned into a museum with manuscripts, photos and paintings, original furniture, and various of his writing instruments. Dickens lived there briefly between April 1937 and December 1939, a young man, fresh from the fame and income of *The Pickwick Papers* and at the beginning of what turned out to be a most unhappy marriage to Catherine Hogarth. The explanations on the wall of one room reveal some of the details of that relationship, including his feelings for his sister-in-law Georgina and his later-years relationship with the young actress, Ellen Terry. Oh, those Victorians. The museum opened in 1925 after the house was threatened with demolition.

The
CHARLES DICKENS
MUSEUM

Woburn Walk

Just off Upper Woburn Place and a block from Euston Road, Woburn Walk was designed by Thomas Cubitt in 1821 as London's first pedestrian street. It's not very long, just a single block with bow-fronted buildings on either side.

WILLIAM BUTLER YEATS
IRISH POET AND DRAMATIST
LIVED IN THIS HOUSE
THEN KNOWN AS 18 WOBURN BUILDINGS
FROM 1895 TO 1919

Though fashionable in its prime, Woburn Walk now seems to be in low-rent area, home to small shops and take-out places like Woburn Tandoori and Wot the Dickens. But W.B. Yeats lived on the street between 1895 and 1919.

Fitzroy Square

This quiet, attractive square in Bloomsbury contains the house, number 29, that was the home of Virginia Woolf from 1907 through 1911. George Bernard Shaw lived there first, between 1887 and 1898.

According to "Socialism in Bloomsbury: Virginia Woolf and the political aesthetics of the 1880," an article by Ruth Livesey in the *2007*

Yearbook of English Studies, Woolf rejected the pragmatic socialism of Shaw and Beatrice Webb, preferring instead the aesthetic socialism of William Morris. If that is so, Woolf's ideological disagreement certainly didn't affect her personal relationship with Shaw, at least, if we can believe what she told him in a typewritten letter of 15th May 1940. It begins, "Your letter reduced me to two days silence from sheer pleasure." In fact, she confesses to having fallen in love with him (no doubt metaphorically) when they met at the Webbs' despite her intention to resist him. "But in a jiffy you made me re-consider all that and had me at your feet." She notes that "you have acted a lover's part in my life for the past thirty years," thus going back to 1910. And she extends an open invitation to visit her and Leonard in their home of the time at 37 Mecklenburgh Square. Perhaps they shared memories of living at number 29—the efficiency of the fireplaces, the functioning of plumbing.

A number of other notables made their homes in Fitzroy Square: The Pre-Raphaelite painter Ford Madox Brown lived at 39. Roger Fry's Omega Workshop occupied 33, a design enterprise founded in 1939 by members of the Bloomsbury Group, including the artist and critic Roger Fry, Virginia's sister Vanessa Bell and her artist lover—after her affair with Fry—Duncan Grant, as well as Wyndham Lewis, who left early to set up the rival Rebel Art Centre. Grant had lived at 21 in 1909 before the Omega Workshop. William Archer, a theater critic and collaborator of Shaw's, at 27. More recently Ian McEwan made his home in the square and used it as a setting in his 2005 novel, *Saturday.*

One might think those London wanderings would have prepared me better if—in a grotesque nightmare—I had to retake all those Brit lit exams. But I'd probably read the questions and lose myself in daydreams of places, all those pictures in my head.

WATCH OUT FOR THE HIPPOS, MR. KENNEDY! A Short Happy Safari in South Africa

Thomas E. Kennedy

> "The lion still stood looking majestically and coolly toward this object that his eyes only showed in silhouette, bulking like some super-rhino . . . Then
> . . . he saw a man figure detach itself from it . . ."
> —Ernest Hemingway, "The Short Happy Life of Francis Macomber"

AFTER TWO HOURS IN A SWEATY, dusty, banged up SUV from Pretoria airport to the Honeyguide camp, I snicker when the woman in the check-in tent has us sign disclaimers that we will take no legal action against the camp in the event that we are mauled, killed or in any way injured by wild animals. It was my idea that this area outside of Kruger Park in the northeastern part of South Africa would be a kind of variant of Disneyland, a realistic one, but not to include mauling animals.

We are instructed sternly never to return alone in the dark from mess to our sleeping tent without being accompanied by one of the rangers—there is danger of encountering an angry dugger boy buffalo. I begin to wonder whether I have been wise inviting my teenaged daughter and son along. Settled in my tent a few minutes later, I hear our travel companion—a six-foot-four-inch 200+ pound Dane named Jesper—holler in alarm that an elephant has stuck its trunk into his tent flap—and I begin to suspect this was not a good idea at all.

We will be two days here in the main camp, touring in a jeep, three days in a bush camp, tracking on foot, then the final day back in the main camp to celebrate—perhaps to celebrate that we are still alive, if indeed we are.

Our travel companion, Jesper, in front of the elephants who have discovered an underground water supply running through plastic pipes into the camp

We will be two days here in the main camp, touring in a jeep, three days in a bush camp, tracking on foot, then the final day back in the main camp to celebrate—perhaps to celebrate that we are still alive, if indeed we are.

The remainder of our first afternoon there is spent relaxing in the sun on the edge of the little pool, our bare feet dangling in the cool water—Jesper, Daniel and myself—drinking bottles of Castle beer and watching half a dozen elephants busy at something or other just outside the camp in a clearing some sixty meters away. One of the elephants is leading the others in some sort of game of tear up the earth with your trunk. Isabel wisely decides it is too hot in the sun and chooses the shade of a little lounge lean-to alongside the bar, drinking tea. Early afternoon by the pool is thirsty work. We three men, ranging in age from 17 (Daniel) to 52 (me), take turns fetching fresh rounds of cold Castles from the bar. After a couple of rounds we figure out why the elephants are digging into the loose earth with their trunks. One of them gets hold of something and steps backwards, tearing it from the ground. A plastic water pipe. Who says elephants are dumb? These ones have figured out that water flows into our camp through buried pipes. Apparently they've decided that if they get hold of the pipe and bring it home with them, they will have a ready steady supply of the wet stuff. They go running off, following their clever leader who has a couple of yards of water pipe tucked into his trunk.

"Think they'll elect a new leader when they get back and find out the water didn't travel with the pipe?" Jesper wonders aloud.

"Want another Castle?" Daniel asks. A neat row of empties along the edge of the pool informs me this will be our sixth. My 17-year-old son appears to be perfectly sober. I feel like a bad Dad.

"Daniel," I say. "How in the world can you drink that much beer?"

He tilts his head quizzically. "Am I not your son, father?"

We sleep well that night after a succulent meal of antelope stew washed back with South African cab, each of us alone on crisp clean sheets in his or her tent, listening to the sounds of the jungle night. Bird cries, the *WA-hoo! WA-hoo!* of a baboon followed by the silencing grunt of a dog leader, the almost subaudible crunch of elephant and buffalo stepping quietly through the bush around our tents.

In the morning we are up early for a breakfast of eggs and warthog bacon and out in the jeeps. Our ranger is a 21-year-old named Brendan from Johannesburg, working for the summer to earn money for his education. He is aided by a tracker named Alfus and equipped with a rifle. If he fires the rifle, he tells us, he will lose his job because that will mean he has led us into danger. This sounds to me like textbook logic; I would prefer to know that he would not hesitate to use the rifle if necessary.

We set out in the jeep—an open truck really with a roll bar (no doubt in case of being turned over by a mad rhino, I think facetiously) and a seat mounted on the left fender in which the tracker sits to watch for game. Soon—much more quickly than I expect—the tracker's hand shoots up, the signal that he has spotted game, and he says, "*N'goni.*" *N'goni*, I learn, is the Xitsonga for lion. And I see that we are already closer to a pair of lion than I ever expected or wanted to be.

It occurs to me that if I had been on a safari with Ernest Hemingway, and he heard me thinking such things, he would have considered me beneath contempt, not even worth mocking in fiction. Of course, I carefully conceal any sign of fear from my children, lest I surrender my tentative hold on patriarchal authority. The lion seem unimpressed by us. The lioness rolls onto her back, exposing her belly, as if to invite a scratch.

"We're fine in the truck," says Brendan. "In the truck, we're a large dangerous animal to them. They respect us. But if you separate from the truck, even stand up or stick your hand out, the lion will see you for what you are."

Indeed, I think, remembering the short happy life of Francis Macomber when the point of view shifts to the lion's, who sees Macomber clearly only when he is out of the jeep. The way I feel at the moment Macomber was a pillar of courage by comparison.

Next there are grazing rhinos, curious giraffe, thirsty lion sipping

from a dam. I grow bolder, seeing that the animals may glance curiously at us but seem basically unaggressive, disinterested mostly. Brendan parks the jeep by the dam so we can stretch our legs. Daniel steps into the tracks left by an elephant that had been there before us for a drink—the print is thigh-high on him.

Brendan enquires about my constant note-taking as he tells about the vegetation and animals and insects. I explain that I'm a writer, and he lights up.

"I was named for a writer. An Irish one. My parents were going to take me home from the hospital without a name but there was an Irish nurse there who said that was bad luck. She suggested 'Brendan.' The name of a great Irish writer, she said, who had died just ten years before."

"Brendan Behan," I say, touched by his openness and trust.

"Yes! That's who! And *you're* a writer. I'll do my best to make the safari as interesting as I can for you!"

Not too interesting, please, I think as he proceeds to lead me to a magic guarri tree, explaining what a good friend this tree is: sprigs of magic guarri placed close to the food keep the flies away and can also be used to swat them off in case that doesn't work. The wood is perfect for a cattie—a catapult, or slingshot—and the ragged edge of a magic guarri twig is perfect for brushing your teeth in the bush.

"Trees are the kindest of the earth's creatures," Brendan tells me. "They stand and wait for your need and let you take without complaint. They feed the elephants and impala, the waterbuck, kudu, giraffe, and give a place for the leopard to drag her prey." He points to the chipped bark of a tree. "See chere, a leopard climbed up with her kill. See how the bark is chipped away by her claws." Then he turns and gestures toward a rocky rise, a weeping werbie tree, explaining how it provides seats for the baboons among the rocks and how the baboon eat the werbie fruit and in turn scatter the seeds in their droppings.

His eye catches something and he turns to the dam where a hippo floats, face just above water while an ox picker bird cleans its snout. "That cher hippo is called Sapo," he says. "He comes up and wanders about at night for vegetables to eat. One time a woman—a nurse, a white woman—tried to beat Sapo on the nose with a broom because he kept stealing her carrots, and just as quick as that, Sapo jumped forward and bit off her arm. Hippo look slow but they're fast."

I gauge Sapo to be about 150 meters out on the dam and wonder how fast.

Halfway into the meadow alongside the dam, Brendan shows me a dead leadwood tree—it looks like a short, ashen-faced man standing stiffly, one rotted up-thrusting branch like an arm raised to get our attention. Even dead, he explains, it provides perches where the buzzards can sleep while they wait for an updraft because the buzzards are so big they have trouble lifting their own weight with muscle. "And what the trees do for men!" he goes on. "Wood for your fire, leaves to heal you—silver cluster leaf to stop you vomiting, common spice leaves for a runny tummy, acacia thorns to pick your teeth and leadwood leaves for toothpaste, boiled knob thorn for a toothache, sour plum tree after too much wine or gin and the soft leaves...," Brendan lowers his voice so Isabel does not hear, "...to wipe your bum."

Brendan has only begun. He proceeds to tell of the many things he could do with the buffalo thorn: the leaf stops a wound's bleeding and a branch, the natives say, would catch the spirit of the dead if brushed across the place a person fell so you could bring the spirit home to rest in peace. Impala eat buffalo thorn leaves, and an Impala buck has to keep many she's happy. Brendan smiles. "Help a man with that, too."

By now the notebook I thought would last me all week is already half full. I can hardly write fast enough to keep up with young Brendan's enthusiasm and knowledge. While I am still recording the last details he is onto another idea. He is telling Alfus that we should proceed from here on foot because Mr. Kennedy is a writer and they must give me good experiences to write about.

Before I can protest we are many meters from the dam, wading through thigh-high yellow grass, solemnly instructed that we are to walk in single file, that we are to stay together, that we are not to chatter, and that we are to obey the ranger's instructions without hesitation. The file is structured thus: first the tracker, next the rifle-bearing ranger, behind him the guests—Jesper is placed in front of Daniel and Isabel, he to protect them from the front, and I to cover the rear. If we happen upon something dangerous, the tracker will signal by repeatedly flapping the palms of his hands backwards at waist level toward the flank, which means we must step backward rapidly. Under no circumstances are we to turn our backs on a wild animal and absolutely never are we to run away. That is an invitation for the chase.

Before I know it, we set off on foot without the protection of the jeep, wading single file through thigh-high yellow grass

I am wondering what we do if an animal sneaks up behind me, last in the flank, wonder whether that is a dumb question, remember African movies—*King Solomon's Mines,* no doubt—where the last bearer in a flank is suddenly picked off by a hungry cat and goes down yelling, "Aieee...!" One of the cast's expendable characters, good for a shudder of blood lust.

But Brendan is too far ahead at the front of the flank for me to shout out my question with dignity. Anyway, shouting is forbidden. We move forward through the grass at a brisk pace toward a tangle of small trees and bush when suddenly we stop. To my horror, I see palms flapping backwards, just glimpse a lean young lion male lying within the trees, another on his feet to the left of the clearing, eyes burning at us like Blake's Tyger. I manage to snap two pictures before the backward jog reaches me. Although I am last in the flank, I also flap my palms backwards. We are jogging quite swiftly backwards toward the dam, and the two lion are creeping toward us, one off to the left, the other to the right.

Brendan calls back over his shoulder to me, "Mr. Kennedy, just keep an eye open for any hippo in the dam! Don't get close to them!"

Oh, I think, you can be certain I will not.

In the clearing again, we huddle. The jeep is perhaps 200 meters off to our right. I am thinking how nice it would be to have my children and myself safely back in that big-animal-looking vehicle, but Brendan says, "Here's the thing. The one has cut us off and the other is flanking us. He knows we want the jeep and that's the way to get us."

The one lion circles behind us

I glance at Jesper. His eyes seem to reflect my thoughts: We're meat.

"I don't like that they're crawling," Brendan says. "They're stalking us. They're hungry. They're too young to know it's best to stay away from the people."

I'm thinking, I am not Ernest Hemingway nor was meant to be...

"I may have to fire the rifle," says Brendan.

"Can you kill them both?" I ask.

"That would mean my job, and Alfus' job, too," says Brendan. "I'd just hope to scare 'em off."

We all exchange stoic glances as I regret having chosen South Africa over Greece for our vacation, and Brendan begins to make noise with his rifle, cranking the bolt and slamming it shut, smacking his palm hard against the wood of the stock. Alfus is doing a kind of dance in the grass which I very much hope is the right magic. Absurdly, I find my brain humming, *Wim-o-way, Ah wim-o-way...* when Brendan says, "Now they've regrouped behind us, see?"

I don't see—my eyes are shut tight.

"We have a clear path to the jeep."

Across the spongy dam bank and soon we are piling into the beautiful, sturdy, olive-green jeep—truck really, big as a double-rhino, big enough to draw respect from a lion, two lions, even hungry ones. Brendan doesn't start the ignition. He sits there for a moment behind the wheel and Alfus turns back in his tracker's chair and begins to laugh. Brendan laughs, too, and soon we all begin to chortle, belly laugh, and that is when I realize how real the danger was.

As we pull away, Brendan points across to the tree line where a herd of bachelor impala leap off into a run—two hungry lions close behind, no doubt.

"They taste better than us," says Brendan. "You'll see."

For lunch there is impala pie in hot onion sauce, and after lunch we learn that Brendan has been reprimanded for putting us in harm's way. The story spreads, and no one is taken out that afternoon, we stay in the main camp. At dinner—zebra steaks in mushroom gravy—the other guests enquire with ill-concealed envy if it is true we were stalked by two lion today. Clearly they are disgruntled, feel *they* are not getting their money's worth. *They* did not get to go out on foot. *They* were not stalked by lion.

The leader of the camp, a short lean man with a neat brown moustache, asks if we would like a new ranger. Without having to consult, Jesper and I instantly agree we are perfectly happy with Brendan. We definitely want to continue with him. Isabel's apparent great relief is my first clue that other factors are at play here than Brendan's merely wanting to help me gather material for my writing. I am not oblivious to Isabel's beauty.

Next day we stay in or very near the jeep from morning to evening, which suits me fine. It seems we are concentrating on less dangerous game. We see a cut-throat finch, blood red feathers topping its breast, and a brown snake eagle circling overhead and a yellow-faced little bee eater, green coat iridescent in the sun. We see the hole of a baboon spider, big around as a fat plum and sheer as polished pipe; Brendan pours water down the hole, but the spider does not emerge. We hunker down in whispering silence by a jackal pup asleep in a drain pipe which Brendan asks us not to tell about—otherwise the others will come to see it and frighten it and it might run off from its mother who is out hunting for her pup's food. We see bush babies and vervid monkies, waterbuck and zebra, a wild dog with spotted hide and big ears sticking up from the grass.

Across the dam, a lone wildebeest, abandoned by the herd, dances madly, whipping its head in agony from the maggots planted in its brain. In the distance, we hear the bark of a dog baboon and a blacksmith plover clicking overhead, and a giggling lady flies near with a shiver of wings. Brendan shows us where a herd of elephant has passed, dragging their trunks through the dust.

When Brendan spots another tree with leopard claw marks in the bark, he parks and gives Alfus his rifle and tells him to go off to see where the leopard has gone. He wants us to see leopard. While Alfus is gone, we lounge alongside the jeep, waiting, and Brendan says, "You mustn't tell I let Alfus take the rifle. I could lose my job for that, giving the rifle to a black."

It occurs to me that I am concerned—not because Brendan gave the rifle to a black, but because we are sitting here without a rifle to defend ourselves with. I begin to wonder about Brendan's judgment. Still, we have the jeep. Up above the crest of a hill, we see a giraffe running and an ostrich.

"There are not many ostrich any more," says Brendan. "The lion eat them." Then he leads us from the jeep a little way out into the field. "See here," he says, "these are zebra tracks. Running. And see here. A leopard overtook her. The leopard are shy but they are here."

Alfus comes back shaking his head and hands the rifle back to Brendan. I notice that Brendan is as tall as Jesper, though much thinner, and Alfus is shorter than I and has a younger face than I had thought at first. Early thirties perhaps. Brendan checks the chamber of the rifle and slings it on his shoulder.

"It's soon time for a sundowner," he says. "Then back to the camp for dinner. Tomorrow we camp in the bush." He drives the jeep to a water hole the size of a small pond in a clearing that slopes gently like a shallow bowl from all sides. We park. He and Alfus break out the chest with the cool drinks and snacks.

We stand around the jeep, chatting and sipping gin in the gathering dusk, sun stripes pale and low to the ground across the yellow grass and the darkening water of the drinking hole. Abruptly Brendan raises his arm for silence. "Listen," he whispers.

At first I hear nothing, then an almost subaudible slow crunching sound. Brendan gestures with slow caution across the water hole just as the animals step out of the trees—tens, scores of them, hundreds. They keep appearing. Brendan whispers, "This herd has about 400—I saw them on the Riebuck Plane the other day. They drink in order of rank—the bulls first. Look, you can see the last of the sunlight lighting up their eyes as they look across at us."

"Will they charge?" someone asks.

"No. They feel safe in a herd. It's only the strays that are dangerous, the dugger boys. In a herd they feel safe and would run from a sneeze back into the safety and comfort of the herd, powerful as they are. The dugger boys will charge without warning, and they don't mock charge either like most big animals. They won't tolerate anything getting too close. See that bull there, how he raises his nose to smell us. Stay close to the jeep."

When the first wave of the bulls have drunk their fill, the next takes their place in the water, and the lead animals head slowly for the trees again. How lightly they step for an animal that weighs fifteen hundred pounds. Awed, we watch the quiet, orderly procession of enormous animals disappear back into the trees, leaving the empty landscape behind them, as though they had never been there, had been an illusion, a dream of buffalo in the dusk.

Water buffalo take a sundowner

Next day, we are in the bush where conditions are more primitive than the main camp—no roomy tents with private sinks and toilets and crisp folded sheets. Here was more like the army, though the tents were mounted on foot-high platforms to discourage crawling intruders. The shower consists of a suspended bucket with a watering can spout mounted in the bottom, and the toilet is porcelain but doesn't flush and is out in the open, behind the tents. Sitting on the bowl, you look down to the dry pit of the river bed below, dotted with fresh elephant droppings, bright brown and orange, melon-shaped balls and hyena spoor, white from the bones they eat, crushing them with their powerful jaws.

The bush staff consists of cooks and trackers and, of course, ranger Brendan. We dine in a mess tent, a canvas overhead mounted on four poles, a wood platform for a floor beneath our canvas chairs. We are served by Moses, who has cooked on an open campfire off behind us.. Brendan eats with us beneath the canvas ceiling. After he has served, Moses joins the black staff to eat seated on rocks and vehicle running boards around the cooking fire. I ask about that, and Brendan tells me, "They prefer to. Sometimes they invite me to join them and laugh because I use a fork instead of my fingers."

Bush tent

We sit long after dinner, drinking gin and beer, talking by the flickering kerosene lamp, watching shadowy elephant circle by, snapping trees for night snacks, huge black shadows against the blue and green darkness of the jungle night.

Brendan tells us that the name the trackers have given him in Xitsonga is *Mariban*d, which means one too cool to lose his temper. But that is close to another word, *maraband*, which means one who eats too much, so he has to listen carefully to be sure he is not being teased.

It is very dark, nearly ten. We have to rise early next morning. Daniel and I are sharing a tent, and I suggest we turn in.

"I'll stay up a little longer, Dad," says Isabel. Brendan says nothing, nor does he move or look at me.

"Okay, Isabel. Ten minutes, right?"

"Fifteen."

"I'll be sure she reaches her tent safely,Mr. Kennedy, " says Brendan.

We light our way back to the tent by flashlight, alert to the possibility of dugger boys. Daniel retires and is soon snoring away in whatever dreams this day has inspired. I sit at the little table on the wooden platform outside the tent, shining the beam of the flashlight onto my watch from time to time. I can see the flickering kerosene lamp in the mess tent perhaps seventy-five meters away. I hear the burbling of a zebra, off in the distance the bark of a dog baboon. Brendan has trained our ears well. At ten-thirty, I step out to the path and follow my flashlight beam down to the mess tent where Brendan and Isabel sit alone on either side of the table, speaking softly.

"Better come to bed now, Bel," I say. "It's late." And to Brendan, "Thanks for a terrific day, Brendan."

"My pleasure, Mr. Kennedy," he pipes, and I follow Bel back to her tent, wishing I could be less of a stereotype.

Our last day in the bush, we drive to the Riebuck Plane. On the way we see two bull giraffe square off to fight for leadership of the herd, swinging their necks at one another's belly, gouging with skull horns. Much of the fight passes in stillness and glaring. I am unable to determine which of them, if either, is winning.

We reach the Riebuck Plane about noon and set out on foot, single file through the trees. Brendan explains that we'll follow an animal path which is a truer path, does not swerve around thorn bushes as a human path would. When we have hiked for fifteen or twenty minutes we come to the edge of a broad yellow clearing. The sun is high overhead. Sweat rolls from beneath my cap, down my back. There is nothing in the clearing other than a broad, round, chest-high bush about a third way across. The tree line on the other side is perhaps a hundred or hundred-fifty meters away. Brendan signals that we should follow him across. I'm hoping that we will see no *n'goni* here.

Nearly a third way across, almost at the bush, two white rhino step out of the tree line on the other side and pause perhaps seventy meters away. Brendan signals us to stop. Should we move back? "They're too fast for us," he whispers. "And if we start moving they'll know we're here and might go for us. A rhino hits full speed in three strides and full speed is forty miles an hour. But they can't see us. They *look* like they can, but they can't. They're almost blind. But if the wind changes, we're in trouble. They'll smell us." He looks at me. "If that happens, you all get down on your bellies under the edge of that bush. They'll smell you but they won't know what you are."

This sounds dubious, but I can think of no alternative. "Daniel," I whisper. "I'll cover Isabel. Can you manage yourself?"

"Yeah," he whispers back.

Then we are silent. We watch the two big animals. I can feel a light breeze on my forehead. Then suddenly it riffles my hair from behind, and the two rhino heads swing toward us in one swift movement.

None of us speaks but Isabel, who says, "*Shit!*"

They start forward in a side by side charge. I'm poised to scoop Isabel under the bush, too frightened to feel my fear, thinking, Why doesn't Brendan shoot? But he is only making noise with the rifle, rattling the bolt, smacking the stock as Alfus dances about like a wasp on a doughnut. But the rhino are on stride three, maybe thirty meters away and moving fast as an automobile. The ground rumbles with their charge. Alfus has his cattie out and is firing stones now. The rhino are about twenty-five meters from the bush when one of Alfus' stones strike the underbelly of the bull. In unison they change direction in a ninety-degree turn and head for the trees to our right.

Brendan smiles at me. "You know that thing about hiding under the bush? I never actually tried it, but I heard it works."

That night in camp there is much laughter. Alfus has his cattie out to show it, and he is laughing, too.

"Can I try that?" Brendan asks and takes the slingshot, loads it with a stone and draws back the rubber sling. Suddenly he turns, aiming it at Alfus' leg. Alfus chuckles. At the last moment, Brendan swings away and fires his stone at the wooden water tank. He hits it but the rubber sling recoils, smacking his hand so he yelps and drops the cattie. Alfus chuckles again and retrieves the weapon as the ranger cools his stung fingers in the air. Alfus loads and fires at the trunk of a tall slender tamboeti tree. The stone whacks the bark, chipping it. He quickly loads and fires again, slicing off a cluster of ticking seeds that fall and lay twitching on the earth, eager to release their blood-sucking larvae.

Jesper and I want Alfus to join us for drinks that evening, but he stays with his own while the four of us celebrate with gin and whisky and beer the continuing fact of our existence.

Next day we tip Moses and Brendan well, and we tell Brendan if there is any trouble at all about the rhino to lay the blame on us, that we insisted.

On the airplane home to Copenhagen, lifting up over the yellow landscape below, patches of green, mountain, river, blue lake and dam, I cannot help but wonder if I really experienced the days I am leaving behind there. A zoo will never again do it for me. I flip through my note pad, completely filled with my scribble and augmented by many extra sheets folded into quarters so they could fit in my back pocket. The stewardess comes with drinks. I take out a legal pad, let down my table as a writing desk. And I begin to write a short story.

The story is about a hero—the hero of our safari—Alfus.

Under the title "Young Lion across the Water," this has been published in *Prism International* and in *Atlas, An International Paperback Magazine of New Writing, Art & Image.*

A HAPPY DAY-NURSERY
Gloomy Icelandic Fictions

Walter Cummins

ALL WE KNEW ABOUT REYKJAVIK came from friends who owned an apartment there and others who had been quick-visit tourists. The city had a reputation among the young of Europe and the U.S as a great place to party, pulsating to the sounds of native rock bands. We knew three women who went there for a week of drinking, the highlight of their stay the night they closed a restaurant with the owner joining their ongoing celebration. All that alcohol reminded me of tales told by a friend stationed miles from the city on an American air force base in the sixties. When they weren't flying, all they did to fill the time was drink in the BOQ. It must have been catching. During the trip over, some in-flight reading revealed that seven percent of Icelandic males had been in rehab facilities. According to Alcoholics Anonymous World Headquarters, Iceland is the western country with the highest number of AA groups per capita was Iceland. Does all that summer daylight and winter darkness have something to do with it?

Icelanders also have the reputation of being big readers, devouring books as much as they do booze. Figuring that imbibing alone wouldn't prepare me for the trip, I decided to read translations of Icelandic novels and watch Icelandic movies. Drunkenness abounded. Along with bleak destructive behavior, acts of betrayal, and dysfunctional families. Yet on the most recent world happiness scale Icelanders rank near the top, according to the United Nations Development Programme's (UNDP) Human Development Index.

John Carlin, in the May 18, 2008 issue of Britain's *The Observer,* opens with a litany of statistics that would seem to argue against happiness:

> Highest birth rate in Europe + highest divorce rate + highest percentage of women working outside the home = the best country in the world in which to live. There has to be something wrong with this equation. Put those three factors together –loads of children, broken homes, absent mothers – and what you have, surely, is a recipe for misery and social chaos. But no.

Beyond leading the world in book buying, enjoying near the longest life expectancy and per capita income, saving energy with volcanic thermal heating, and breathing pristine air, the most essential reason for this well being, according to Carlin, is "the hardy self-confidence that defines individual Icelanders, which in turn derives from a society that is culturally geared—as its overwhelming priority—to bring up happy, healthy children, by however many fathers and mothers."

Yet the people who populate the novels and the films are far from self-confident, wallowing in their misery. And the question of parentage figures prominently in a number of the stories. Perhaps it's a matter of happy families being so alike they're not worth reading about. Or perhaps it's a curiosity about others, say, awful Americans in Ice-

landic clothing. But googling, I did run across a study of borderline personality-disordered alcoholics in Iceland. They may provide the supply of fictional archetypes.

101 Reykjavik is both a novel by Hallgrímur Helgason and a film directed by Baltasar Kormákur that won the Discovery Film Award at the Toronto International Film Festival. 101 is the postcode for the city center where rows of small houses, many covered with corrugated metal, line the side streets leading into the main shopping street, Laugavegur, which was accurately described to me as "about the size of an alley." The anti-hero protagonist, Hlynur, lives in one of those metal-sided houses with his mother and her female lover, Lolla. Seeing the film before I saw the city, I assumed that architecture was an aberration, suggesting the jerrybuilt dwellings of the world's shantytowns. Not at all. In Reykjavik, they're commonplace. At least in the original city.

Today along the waterfront and in the areas around the center dozens of milti-story apartment buildings are under construction. No one in Hlynur's world lives in them, but there is a scene in the ultramodern Hallgrimskirkja church that literally towers over the city and that, during our visit, was covered in scaffolding.

Judged objectively, Hlynur should be despised or, at least, disliked by readers. (The film softens him by excising several of his more heinous actions.) A 30-year-old do-nothing, he milks the society's social support system and spends his endless free time watching porn, getting high on alcohol or ecstasy, and dallying in aimless sex. Of his homeland he says, "Iceland is a wind-beaten asshole and Icelanders are the lice on its edge." Therefore, "Licelanders." He also evaluates the sex appeal of every woman he meets or fantasizes about in kroner, the full list appended in four pages at the end of the book, from kr 100 for a couch potato mother to kr 4,700,000 for Pamela Anderson. Eve and the Virgin Mary place near the very top of the list. Many of the prices he places are cruel, as are the way he treats real people. But the wit and energy of his first-person narration (translated into English by Brian FitzGibbon) can win over the reader. He describes ugly behavior in a compelling rush of words, often pages of them without a paragraph break.

Pregnancy figures at the center of the plot. Hlynur impregnates Hófi during a bored encounter that gives neither of them pleasure. He sabotages his sister's birth control pills, and she ends up pregnant. His mother, Berlind, and the younger Lolla decide they want a child. Is the source of the seed a surrogate male friend or Hlynur, who engages in mutual drunken seduction with his mother's lover after both overindulge at a New Year's Eve party. It's the most spectacular sexual experience of his life, the language of the description all fireworks.

> ... The sky erupts into a constellation of birthmarks. The silence in the navel of the explosion when she comes. The stillness in the eye of the cyclone ... when I come. I come and, for a moment, everything brightens in a flash, a fireball lighting up the atmosphere and several continents below, before dissolving. And vanishing. What becomes of the sperm?

Alcohol and pregnancy. But these aren't happy Icelanders comfortably casual about who fathered whom. Hófi has an abortion, Hlynur's sister a miscarriage. But Lolla delivers a child and, at the end, Hlynur, hoping it is his, bonds with the baby. A certain level of happiness, though for some readers, given his amoral legacy of indifference and destructiveness, the conversion may not be convincing.

About one-third of the 330,000 Icelanders live in Reykjavik, the remainder scattered in towns and villages around the coast of the Island. A film called "The Sea" depicts a family in one of those fishing villages – a father, Thordur, in possession of an official permit to harvest an annual quota for the sea; his current wife who is the sister of his deceased wife; his two sons and one hostile daughter of the first marriage; his snarling octogenarian mother; a young woman "cousin"; his grandson addicted to video games; and the visiting pregnant French girlfriend of the younger son. There's also the father's mortal enemy, another fishing boat owner and one-time rival for the first wife; a bank manager who is having an affair with the older son's angry wife; an incompetent policeman named Bobo; and a fuzzy black ram that roams freely through the village, to Bobo's great frustration. The ram comes out as the most likeable of the lot.

The village certainly is bleak, and the family fish factory must reek of fish heads and innards. Still, it's not justification for the family's behavior. If these characters had been real people, they alone would have plunged Iceland's rating deep into the pits of the happiness scale. As Stephen Holden wrote in his *New York Times* review, "If ever there were a movie to gladden the hearts of misanthropes, this is it." He also notes, "The shabby village hardly fits the popular image of Iceland as a gleaming, pristine land of glaciers, hot springs and sleek modern architecture . . ."

Unlike the tolerance with which the great majority of Icelanders treat divorce and illegitimacy, Thordur's family seethes with resentment, especially because he was carrying on with his sister-in-law while his wife was suffering through the years of slow, painful dying. To turn another screw, Thordur and his second wife have hidden the fact that he fathered with her the so-called cousin, Maria. Unfortunately, Maria is in love with the youngest son, Agust, home from Paris where he pretended to be working toward a degree in business while really writing songs and finding the spare time to impregnate the beautiful Françoise. Maria manages to seduce Agust during a naked midnight swim in one of those ubiquitous thermal swimming pools. When they learn it's incest, she doesn't care, but he reacts with horror. At the film's climax, Agust torches his father's fish factory, causing the old man's stroke. Agust and Françoise fly back to Paris, and all the others live miserably ever after.

Arnaldur Indridason's *Jar City* is characterized "A Reykjavik Thriller," though it's more of a procedural mystery with a number of clever and satisfying plot twists. While the book offers a map of central Reykjavik and another of the wider area with the routes to suburbs that figure in the story, the reader doesn't get a sense of the city, probably because the prose, outside of dialogue, is just a series of generic declarative sentences, such as: "Elin had stood up and was pacing the room in a frenzy. Erlendur sat tight and had sunk deeper into the soft armchair."

Erlendur, a detective with the local police, enters on the opening page after a body of a 70-year-old man is found on the floor an apartment. As expected, the mystery broadens and comes to involve Iceland's genetic research as well as several variations of the parent-child relationship, including the products of rape. Even divorced Erlendur's estranged daughter, Eva Lund, a down and out drug addict, becomes pregnant. There is a son he never sees, though Eva Lund turns up at his apartment begging for money and shouting abuse.

The Jar City of the title refers to a secret collection of vessels containing human organs salvaged from autopsies in past years. The solution to the mystery hinges on recovering the brain of a long-dead child for evidence of a genetic defect that leads to the murderer. The detection moves from the old-fashioned jars to the studies being conducted by the Genetic Research Centre. I don't know if such a collection as Jar City ever existed, but the genetic research is certainly real. And controversial.

In 2000, the government created a national health database, at first to contain medical and family histories. When the mission was expanded to include genetic information, opponents emerged from fear of privacy violations, abuse of the findings, genetic stereotyping, and a monopoly by big business. In fact, the parliament granted exclusive access to the health records to a biomedical company called deCODE genetics, which in turn signed an agreement with the pharmaceutical firm Hoffman-LaRoche that was seeking the genes related to more than 30 diseases, include heart conditions, emphysema, and Alzheimer's.

What makes Iceland ideal for such studies is its small size and homogeneous population, the great majority of which, 80 percent, can be traced on family trees for many generations. The country is also very isolated geographically and, until recently, has had little immigration that would introduce new genes. As a result, people with a common disease can have their DNA investigated through a genealogical database for possible genetic causes.

One common denominator found among the societies at the top of the list of the world's happiest people is homogeneity. Indridason turns that advantage into the source of brutal murders, the crime having been committed by the initial victim's son, a product of rape who has inherited a deadly genetic flaw that lay dormant in his parent. When he discovers the identity of the man who fathered him and the young half sister who died years before of the same disease, he takes revenge.

These novels and films, in their obsession with parentage and family connections, play on the obverse of the very characteristics that have brought about the happiness of the Icelanders' lot. The extent of the misery depicted may be all imaginary. As one website notes, "Iceland is about as safe as a country can possibly get. The murder rate is close to zero."

Iceland's Nobel Prize author Halldór Laxness, who died in 1998 at age 95—another testament to the longevity of his people—wrote the novel *The Atom Station* in 1948. At that time, just a few years after Hiroshima and Nagasaki, he, like millions of others, feared the Bomb and the end of civilization. Laxness himself was in the midst of his pro-Russian Communism phase and hostile to the West, especially to American pressures to establish nuclear bases on Iceland, which had received independence from Denmark just a few years before on June 17, 1944. Laxness considers Parliament's decision to accept the bases an act of selling the country. But, despite this issue and the book's title, the real theme is a contrast of the decadence of life in Reykjavik, particularly among the affluent capitalists and politicians, and the pure north of the island, were wild ponies roam, nature is pure, and the spirit of the Sagas still prevails. The novel is narrated by Ugla, a young woman from the north who arrives in the city to serve as a maid in the home of the Member of Parliament representing her home area.

Though the novel addresses a number of social and political themes that satirize the urban hoi polloi, pregnancy and children become central to the plot. Those of the parliamentarian and their equally rich cousins, progeny of the Prime Minister, are drunken vandals and sexually promiscuous. The beautiful elder daughter, called Dudu by her mother and Fruit-blood by Ugla, at fourteen becomes impregnated by a much older married man. Ugla, pregnant herself from a one-night encounter with a policeman also from the north, tells the girl her father probably will ship her off to America to have the baby and avoid scandal:

> Genteel people with morals and sensitive nerves send their daughters abroad when they get into trouble, even though uncouth people like us don't understand that sort of thing and just have our children where we are.

Instead of to America, the girl's father sends her for an abortion: "He pushed irons up me. He killed me. There were bloody shreds of something in the bowl." Ulga, in contrast, goes home to her parents to deliver her daughter: "When my mother showed her to me I felt I did not know her, but I felt a little fond of her at once because she was so little and large. And my father, who never laughs, laughed when he saw her."

Ugla's child represents of a broader issue involving children, the building of a day-nursery in Reykjavik. The Town Council first defeated the proposal because it was a Communist idea and because such a nursery would lead to an increase in sexual immorality. Nurseries, those in power argue, should exist only in the home of true Christians and those of decent morals. "Why," Ugla asks, "should there not be nurseries for the children of non-true Christians with wicked morals, such as me?"

It's clear whose side Laxness is on. Finally, the day-nursery is approved and Ugla chooses to unite with the father of her child and stay in Iceland despite the fact that it, like the rest of the world, has become an atomic station. If the Bomb came, there would be refuge among the fjords, streams, mountain tops, and wild ponies— the world of the Sagas.

In 1948, Laxness considered only those in Iceland's rustic north truly happy. Now happiness has spread through the land, and it's all a day-nursery. But novelists and film makers scorn.

THE VIRGINS

Thomas E. Kennedy

> "The Danish flag waves from poles everywhere.There are Danish buildings. There are Danish cannons. There are Danish signs. There are even Danes."
>
> —*A Tour to the Danish West Indies* (in Danish), by Kenneth Bo Jørgensen, Copenhagen: Politikens Publishing House, 2006

THE IDEA SEEMED SIMPLE and modest enough: to have a couple of weeks relaxation in a near-tropical paradise. Blue skies, turquoise sea, sun, snorkeling, pool swims, rum and papaya, Caribbean chicken-stew, crabcakes, iguana-watching, a little reading, maybe even a bit of writing. Because Lady Alice is Danish and I have lived more than half of my sixty-three years in Denmark, the Virgin Islands seemed the obvious candidate—those three Virgins which for most of 251 years had been Danish, only since 1917 American.

Our preparation was lackadaisical. We watched the Danish feature film from 1987 about the 19th century Virgin Islands Governor, Peter von Scholten. (One of the film's highlights was that the character of General Buddo, leader of the slaves, was played by the American bluesman Dale Smith, who has been living in Denmark for decades.) Von Scholten defied his king in 1848 when, to stop an uprising in progress, he decreed freedom for the slaves on St. Thomas, St. John, and St. Croix; the king had absurdly wanted to grant freedom only for newborns, creating a situation where the children of adult slaves would be free. I allowed myself to assume the Von Scholten story meant that things were A-okay with Danish-VI relations. Amazing how one can allow oneself such less than semi-conscious assumptions about a former colony. Anyway, it was a vacation, not an historical tour.

Other than that, I dipped into *Politikens* travel guide and got the impression of blue-eyed joy and even-teethed smiles as Danish flags still decoratively fluttered in the island breezes from the historical colonial Danish buildings, cozy Danish street names, and a general mood of I'm okay-you're okay, let's divvy up this post-colonial Eden.

After a long flight from Copenhagen via Paris and Atlanta, we arrived at Cyril E. King Airport on St Thomas and were transported to our beautiful, spacious, Point Pleasant apartment on the east part of the island, with a broad terrace overlooking Sugar Beach. What could be more sugar-sweet and pointedly pleasant than that?

Sugar Beach, our naively named private paradise for two weeks

We lazed for a few days before getting the itch to explore, bought a tour, were taxied to Red Hook and ferried across the bouncing sparkling blue waves of Pillsbury Sound to Cruz Bay on the neighboring island of St John, population 4,000, including 147 taxi drivers and a great many schoolchildren who wear different colored uniforms from school to school, which colors provide for the demarcation of their war zones—reds against blues against greens with pocket knives and the occasional pistol. Why do they do this? Perhaps it has something to do with the servicing of nearly two million wealthy tourists a year, sailed in on cruise ships, pockets deep with money for the purchase of duty-free items the locals will never have—diamonds, rubies, white and red gold, tanzanites, Cartiers, Swiss watches, Belgian chocolates... On St Croix, the violence against cruise-ship tourists had increased to the point that the ships have dropped the island from their itinerary.

At the dock in Cruz Harbor, we were led to a fire-engine red, open-sided bus and delivered to the charge of our tour guide, Clyde, an eggplant black, burly, muscular man with gold-star inlays glinting from his few remaining teeth. Clyde began by telling us that he is the father of nine. "Would ha' be the twelve apostle, but three die on me."

Clyde of St. John

There were fifteen of us in his gleaming little bus, and he offered the prize of a free drink to whoever could guess our first stop on the tour.

No one won the drink; the correct response was "the ladies room," a necessary preliminary to a two-hour tour of the national park.

"Later," he explained, "You men got to give de ladies yo plastic money. De wimins love to buy ting. And when de wimin do dat, de men loves to go drink some rum." This was the first of a running stream of sexist jokes about Eden and poisonous fruit, the greed of women and the need for Dagwood-Bumstead compliancy in men.

For some reason he then said, "I hope you all Americans!" Which startled me. Lady Alice is a Dane and was not treated with unequivocal kindness by the guardians of the American perimeters at our point of entry in Atlanta.

The questions: *Have you ever engaged in moral turpitude, espionage, been convicted of a crime, declared insane, are you visiting the US for the purposes of prostitution, have you recently visited a farm, are you carrying any plants or seeds or animal products? If yes, please explain...* And to top it off, because the temperature when we arrived on St Thomas was predicted to be in the 90s, we left Atlanta dressed light; Lady Alice, being Danish body and soul, had dressed in a light zip-up jacket without a stitch beneath. Naturally, she did not remove the jacket to send it along the conveyer belt through the x-ray machine. As she passed through the magnetic arch, she was stopped by a tall, angular, cool-eyed female African American security officer who gave me The Hand when I tried to follow Lady Alice. I stopped, still within earshot.

"Please go back, remove your jacket and place it on the belt, ma'am."

"That would be embarrassing," said Lady Alice. "I have nothing underneath."

The officer gawked. "*Nothin'*! Honey, this is *America*! We be usin' *underwear*! Oh, go on!" and signalled me through.

And although I am still an American citizen, vote in federal elections and file an American income tax return every year, after thirty-two years abroad, I sometimes forget whether I am American or Danish in any given situation. Thus, Clyde's question startled me.

"Do foreigners need passports to get into the national park?" I blurted. "We're Danes."

Clyde's eyes narrowed. I had broken the rhythm of his patter. He said, "You Danes got dese islands from the English as a gift to de Danish king. Then we bought them from you in 1917 fo' a big bag of gold. Then de Germans take you land from you in 1940 because you could not fight to defend youself." He dropped into a boxing stance. "Muhammed Ali would never give up so fast. We had to come and free you." He lifted his chin and showed the gold stars in his teeth. "But for today let us say you Americans like all de others here."

He then made a roll call of who was from which of the many great cities of the US of A, commenting on the virtues and weaknesses of the various sports teams from each, pronouncing himself the uncle of Michael Jordan, and spicing his banter with various sexist jokes he seemed to presume we would all find hilarious. Not many joined the smattering of polite laughter.

Although my knowledge of the history of these Virgin Islands was rudimentary, I was aware of the inaccuracies in Clyde's account. My guide book time-line showed that after their discovery by Columbus in 1493, the islands had changed hands between the Spanish, French and Knights of Malta, but had been primarily Danish from 1666 to 1917, only very briefly British and finally, only after 424 years, American. Further, the Danish sale to the US was partially to help avoid the Germans seizing them as a stronghold to the south of the States during World War I. And finally, there had been good reasons for the Danish capitulation to the Germans in 1940 which even Mohammed Ali and Mike Tyson, battling back to back, could not have overcome, and Denmark had not been liberated in 1945 by the Americans but by the British, rather by the Allies, after some years of increasing resistance by the Danes against the occupiers. Thanks to the Danish resistance, a couple of hundred thousand German troops had been kept busy occupying Denmark and thus prevented from joining the easter or western fronts against the allies. Lady Alice herself had been the victim of a bombing (so called "friendly fire") in 1945 when she was five years old (cf, *The Literary Review*, 49:2:2006, pp 23-48).

But I held my tongue in favor of considering Clyde's apparent antipathy for Danes. Aside from the recent Muhammed cartoon controversy—generally called "the Danish cartoons," although they originated from a single, right-wing Danish newspaper—Danes are accustomed to being liked as a nation and as individuals. It was interesting that Clyde did not seem much to like us.

A closer reading of my Politiken guide book gave good indication of why, and I really had no excuse for not knowing, my ignorance like that of a good German. To my mind, the slave traders had been Dutch and English, the buyers American. In fact, the Danes had also perpetrated their share of this infamy.

Somehow we manage to continue to have our stitlted views of

the world, of elegant mint-julep colonial days, ubi sunt Gone with the Wind, of paradisial islands, swashbuckling Errol Flynn and Johnny Depp pirates. Few places are the facts so bald as in the Danish history of these three islands. This had been no budding new world of experimental democracy. This had been an economic machine to produce wealth for the Danish kingdom, and the machine was fueled by the power of human bodies purchased from unscrupulous tribal chiefs in Ghana for rifles, gun powder, spirits and textiles, packed by the hundreds into the holds of ships and sailed on the western trade winds to the islands where they were sold primarily for sugar, which was transported on the northerly trade winds to Denmark, refined by Danish workers (whose lives were perhaps only marginally quantitatively better than the African slaves'), and the ship was restocked with rifles etc. to be carried by the southern trade winds back to Ghana. This triangular route, at its height, carried 75,000 African slaves a year to the Americas—not counting the fifteen percent who died in transport on the ships. By 1850, the total was 12-15 million Africans, about half to the Caribbean, the remainder divided between North and South America. Kenneth Bo Jørgensen tells us that Denmark's portion of this total was about a hundred thousand Africans, which at the time corresponded to the population of the Danish capital, Copenhagen. Only a small fraction of the total, but enough that Denmark today is calculated to have been the seventh most profitable slave-trade nation.

If one steps back from this segment of the bigger picture, of course, it is difficult to lay specific blame on Denmark. The Caribbe Indians around 1000 AD took the islands from their oginal inhabitants, the reportedly peaceful Taino branch of the Arawaki who had been here since about 300 AD. The Caribbes are said to have enslaved and eaten the Tainos and were in turn themselves massacred five hundred years later by the dreaded Europeans who then proceeded to repopulate the islands with captured African slaves.

To paraphrase Jørgensen's account, the slaves were traded like cattle in market, were fatted in the weeks leading up to the auctions and forced to drink rum to make them seem docile and happy. At the auctions they were made to jump and dance to demonstrate their vitality and were inspected by prospective purchasers from head to foot. Their daily lives in the fields started with the blowing of a conch at five a.m. to rouse them for the feeding of the plantation animals after which they were led to the fields to work under the blistering sun for twelve or thireen hours with a single meal break in the middle of

Annaberg Sugar Plantation where kidnapped Africans slaved to sweeten the bitter dram of Denmark

the day. They were expected to cultivate their own food in the form of roots or had to make do with grits. To keep their work tempo up they were whipped by a *bomba*, a black overseer who was himself whipped by a white overseer if he did not keep his slaves sufficiently active with his whip. In the beginning they were considered animals to the extent that not even clothing was provided.

To paraphrase Jørgensen's account, the slaves were traded like cattle in market, were fatted in the weeks leading up to the auctions and forced to drink rum to make them seem docile and happy. At the auctions they were made to jump and dance to demonstrate their vitality and were inspected by prospective purchasers from head to foot. Their daily lives in the fields started with the blowing of a conch at five a.m. to rouse them for the feeding of the plantation animals after which they were led to the fields to work under the blistering sun for twelve or thireen hours with a single meal break in the middle of the day. They were expected to cultivate their own food in the form of roots or had to make do with grits. To keep their work tempo up they were whipped by a *bomba*, a black overseer who was himself whipped by a white overseer if he did not keep his slaves sufficiently active with his whip. In the beginning they were considered animals to the extent that not even clothing was provided.

Conditions of the so-called house slaves were a little better; they took care of all the house work from cleaning to cooking to breast-feeding the children of their white masters, fanning white brows against the heat as well as having the honor of wiping their masters and mistresses backsides with a specially designed straw wisp. A plantation owner might have from five to twenty-five house slaves. Because at the height of slavery in 1800, the proportion of free citizens to slaves was one to ten, brutal systems of punishment were employed against disobedience including the whip, staking of the tongue with a hot poker, and hanging.

These were the conditions of life. No doubt still are. We allow ourselves unforgivably less than semi-conscious assumptions about the world.

In light of this, it occurs to me that in that instant's narrowing glower of Clyde's eyes, he might well have been thinking: *Dane, your great great grandfather claimed to own mine, whipped him, forced him to labor for your country's wealth at no payment beyond a miserable mid-day meal, brought him into the house to literally wipe white asses. And you know what else they did? In the beginning of the last century, in 1905, they took a little six year old boy back to Denmark on a ship and they put him in a colonial exhibition in the Tivoli Gardens. And when he couldn't sit still for it, they put him into a cage and people would stick their fingers in to see if he bite dem. Dey tink he a cannibal child. And den when he grow up, grow elderly, in the year 1977 when he 78 year old, they invite him to come on some TV variety show, and the host, this man name Otto Leisner, he say to that man, You gon sing a Negro spiritual fo' us? What you tink bout dat?*

The after-effect of such wrongs could only smolder for centuries – here, in the continental US, everyplace that the descendants of black slaves look upon the descendants of whites, where the poor look upon the rich who profited off their sweat and pain and blood.

So let me conclude with a nod to Clyde, to his straight-forwardness. His facts were not quite accurate but he had the gist of it right.

The history here was all about sugar – and what a metaphor for the extremes to which human beings will reach to sweeten their bitter cup. Sugar Beach, indeed. Blood beach.

Now when I grumble about what the British did to the Irish and take refuge in the Danish social democracy, I have Clyde to remember. None of us is innocent.

Bibliography

Turen Går til Dansk Vestindien (A Tour to the Danish West Indies), Kenneth Bo Jørgensen. Copenhagen: Politikens Travel Books, 2006 (in Danish).

Peter von Scholten, Danish feature film, produced by Crone Film Production A/S and Metronome Productions A/S in cooperation with the Danish Film Insitute, 1987.

Postcards from Tivoli, documentary film by Nanna Debois Buhl, Produced with support from The Danish Arts Council's Committee for Visual Arts.

IN THE FOOTSTEPS OF JOHNSON AND BOSWELL
Tobermory, the Isle of Mull

Walter Cummins

GETTING TO THE TOWN OF TOBERMORY on the Inner Hebrides Isle of Mull wasn't easy. My wife, Alison, and I had to fly seven hours from Newark International to Glasgow, take a cab to the city's Queen Street station, kill time in a Café Nero across the street from the station, endure a three-hour train ride to Oban through driving gray rain, drag luggage up and down ramps to a Caledonian MacBrayne ferry, bounce about on rough seas in a downpour for close to an hour, stand dripping in a parking lot after debarking at Craignure on Mull while looking for a non-existent taxi, wait for a bus, ride another forty minutes to a drenched parking lot at the edge of Tobermory, gaze up to our hotel atop a hill overlooking the town, wonder how we would get there through the deluge, and finally find an information trailer, where a kind local called a taxi.

Still, our journey, arduous as it was for 21st-century senior citizens, was nothing like the one endured by Samuel Johnson and James Boswell when they toured the Western Isles in 1773, decades before the railroad existed and even longer before heated ferries with lounges and food service crossed

the water. What we did in less than twenty-four hours took them days, starting with horse and carriage from London to western Scotland, then crossings to the islands postponed because of rain and choppy seas, Johnson below deck with sea sickness when they finally got on a boat. Then days spent on horseback to tour Mull and other Inner Hebrides islands. Johnson, in his sixties at the time, was obese and suffering from scrofula, gout, and fits of depression. Boswell notes of Johnson that he was once "fretted to find that his little horse could scarcely support his weight," adding that Johnson suffered a weakness in his knees and could not walk easily. Yet he endured the trip.

Our much briefer and much more limited travels took place two and a half centuries later. But, with the advantage of buses and taxis and paved roads, we were able see quite a bit of Mull, including a side trip to Iona. Johnson and Boswell, over their extended period, visited many homes for lengthy interactions with residents of the islands. Our conversations, all pleasant, were limited to exchanges with cab drivers and food servers and hotel staff. Of course, the internet, satellites, and cable TV gave us access to knowledge of the wider world beyond Mull. YouTube had provided us with advance views of what we would encounter, though they were hardly the real thing.

Long before the option of posting videos, both Johnson and Boswell wrote books about their experiences when they returned to their homes, Boswell *Journal of a Tour to the Hebrides with Samuel Johnson,* LL.D., published in 1775, and Johnson *A Journey to the Western Isles of Scotland*, also published the same year. Although they were together for the entire time, reading the books suggests they went on separate trips, considering what they chose to write about. Boswell—tuning up for *The Life of Johnson* that appeared in 1791 after Johnson's death, and occasionally referring to that anticipated work—appears to have spent much of his time observing Johnson's interactions with

others and transcribing the great man's declarations on life and letters, always referring to him as Dr. Johnson, a man already famous for his dictionary and literary status. Johnson, on the other hand, after stating that Boswell was an amiable companion in his opening paragraph, has little more to say about his amanuensis or his exchanges with those encountered during their travels:

> I had desired to visit the Hebrides, or Western Islands of Scotland, so long, that I scarcely remember how the wish was originally excited; and was in the Autumn of the year 1773 induced to undertake the journey, by finding in Mr. Boswell a companion, whose acuteness would help my inquiry, and whose gaiety of conversation and civility of manners are sufficient to counteract the inconveniences of travel, in countries less hospitable than we have passed.

Johnson—according to Boswell—truly did have a curiosity about the Hebrides a decade before their actual trip, eager to see a totally different system of life from that they had known, hoping "to find simplicity and wildness," expecting "some inconvenience and hardships, and perhaps a little danger," but confident all would be manageable.

Our decision to visit a Hebrides isles was much more spontaneous—first an idea to go someplace new and remote, deciding "Why not the Hebrides?"; then a need to learn the difference between the Inner and the Outer and do a web search on specific islands before picking. It was the photograph of Tobermory harbor that convinced us, the row of colorful buildings along Main Street (A' Phriomh Shraid in Gaelic) and the sailboats anchored in the harbor. The dark brown building towering on a hill turned out to be the Western Isles Hotel, where we had booked a room. Truth to be told, we were thinking of neither Johnson and Boswell nor of their writings about their experiences, certainly not reading them in advance, not even realizing they had preceded us until we visited the Mull Museum on Main Street.

Johnson's book is more a commentary on place, offering literal descriptions, along with a good deal of socio-economic commentary that emphasizes the bleakness of the landscape and the backward

poverty of the people. He didn't think much of the Scots, having said, among other insults, "Knowledge was divided among the Scots, like bread in a besieged town." Boswell, a proud Scot himself, notes the impressive reading collections in the visited homes and the sophistication of their hosts. Johnson didn't mention these books, the hosts knowledge, or his seasickness "(Dr. Johnson grew sick, and retired under cover") or the pretty young married woman who sat on his lap and teased him with a pecking kiss, as he played along with her mild flirtations ("He kept her on his knee some time, while he and she drank tea"). Boswell, on the other hand, found the scene amusing and Johnson a good sport.

Johnson and Boswell, who would have envied our forty-five minutes on the water in Caledonian MacBrayne comfort, spent hours in the dark, when they crossed from the isle of Coll to Mull. Johnson euphemizes that "we spent the night not very elegantly or pleasantly in the vessel."

Johnson calls their port of landing Tobor Morar (the town's Gaelic name is Tobar Mhoire, meaning "Mary's well") and concludes that it existed for "the security of ships," admitting them "through narrow channels into a bason [sic] sufficiently capacious." While ships were safe, he warns of the winds issuing through the hollows of the mountains with "mischievous violence."

Boswell spells the town Tobermorie. He too praises the excellence of the harbor and also notes the wind storms, in his case specifying that fifteen vessels had been blown from their moorings. What animated him—he quotes Johnson saying, "Boswell is now all alive"—were the

sixty or seventy sailboats from many cities anchored in the harbor: "... the sight of such an assemblage of moving habitations, containing such a variety of people, engaged in different pursuits, gave me much gaiety of spirit." He ascended to the top of a hill for a good view of the harbor, no doubt the same hill we climbed every day to reach our hotel and from which we enjoyed the same prospect, though of a much more developed community and anchorage. Johnson, unlike his enthusiastic companion, was in a bad humor: "he had no joy."

In fact, Johnson seems to have a fixation on duress and hard times. He reports the eight weeks of snow-covered ground during the "black winter" of 1771 and of the unprepared island residents who "could only pine in helpless misery," suffering want and famine. He describes his hours of crossing Mull as an ordeal though a "black and barren" landscape, "a gloom of desolation." He speculates whether care and labor could give nature "a more cheerful face" by the simple task of planting seeds that would grow into trees, then concludes that immediate necessities of life on Mull make such planning for the future impossible: "... in a place, which hardly supplies the craving of necessity, there has been little attention to the delights of fancy."

Throughout Johnson's journey in Mull, he complained that he and Boswell "were always struggling with some obstruction or other, and our vexation was not balanced by any gratification of the eye or mind." Alison and I, in happy contrast, crossed the island on a smooth highway in a taxi that took us through an abundant green-hilled landscape of lakes and evergreens, a scenic pleasure all the way. Our driver, Linus, a Lithuanian émigré who had previously worked on fishing ships and in restaurant kitchens, after just a few years had informed himself of the island's history and natural wonders, as well as perfecting his English. He had turned himself into the ideal guide, pleased to have found life's necessities well provided for on Mull.

If seafood is any measure of comfortable living, Tobermory boasts an abundance fresh from the sea and from a mussel farm on the island. In fact, we couldn't finish the pile of mussels the first time we ordered at Macgochans restaurant, advised by the waitress to pick just the appetizer portion in the future. The Fish Café on a pier at one end of the town's main street had been chosen as the UK's number one fish restaurant a couple of years before our visit. Who had discovered this food so far from everything puzzled me, that and the fact that the restaurant is a humble place with just a few tables and barren décor, where if it had been open in Johnson's time, he would have written that they dined not "very elegantly," though he probably wouldn't have been able to deny the quality of the meal.

Although the notion of going to Tobermory was an accidental discovery for us, the town attracts many visitors because it is considered

one of the prettiest in all Scotland, because the island provides access to viewing wildlife in unspoiled habitat, including the Mull eagle watch, and because it offers several castles, one, Duart, inhabited and open to paying visitors, another a picturesque ruin. The island also includes two locations of standing stores. Food is a bonus, not to mention the single malt whisky available at the Tobermory Distillery, founded in 1798, just a few years after the Johnson-Boswell visit.

Most people arrive with cars brought over by the Caledonian MacBrayne ferry. We were the among the few without vehicles and, as far as we could tell, the only Americans. Yet when Alison told people where we were going at a breakfast one morning, she discovered that her friends Eliot and Millicent had been, the year before, on a cruise through the Hebrides that included several hours in Tobermory. Millicent asked if we would bring a special scent from the soap shop on Main Street. She also revealed that the first foreign movie she ever saw was set on Mull, with a brief scene in the Western Isles Hotel. It was a black and white film from 1945 called *I Know Where I'm Going*, starring Wendy Hiller and Roger Livesey. The hotel displayed a poster advertising the film. We later learned that Livesey, the male lead, never came to Mull because he was performing in a London play. Doubles portrayed his character in long shots, and closeup scenes were enacted in London, then edited in. Unfortunately, Technicolor equipment was scarce in England during the filming in the final months of World War Two.

Not so more recently, when Tobermory became the site of a BBC show for preschoolers titled "Balamory" broadcast between 2001 and 2005 and winning children-show awards. The painted storefronts of the main street are featured, with the child actors wearing clothing of a distinctive color and living in a house of the same color.

Still prominent is the Tobermory cat, the subject of children's books by Debi Gliori and based on a real orange tabby who lives in the town's youth hostel but never appeared during our visit. An ancillary book revealing him in a range of photographs is also for sale. In it, the owner of the seafood trailer parked along the shore complains that the cat, seen perched atop the trailer and a number of cars, eats all his profits. The creator of the feline's fictional persona, Angus Stewart, claims that the cat is "famous for being famous." (The Tobermory cat is a deliberate parody of Donald Trump from his TV celebrity days, even living in T.C. Towers and indulging in a garish life style.) Johnson, whose cat Hodge is famous for being Johnson's cat, in our time probably would have been the subject of such manufactured commercial fuss.

Despite the fact that the Isle of Mull measures three hundred square miles, it is home to only three thousand people, more than half of whom live in Tobermory, the rest clustered in small villages, most along the miles of coastline.

Our informative trip in Linus' taxi took us across the landscape to a tiny place called Fionnphort on the southwestern edge of the island, starting point of the ten-minute ferry trip to Iona, a much smaller island famed in the history of Christianity for the presence of St. Columba (Irish name Colmcille), who spread the religion to the heathen Picts until his death and burial on Iona in the year 597. People still make pilgrimages to the Iona Abbey and Nunnery, the later now a ruin. In addition to religious sites and nature tours, a visitor may also enjoy the pleasures of a golf course.

As we waited for the ferry in Fionnphort, we wandered amid

the shaggy and very benign Scottish cattle blocking the road just a few feet from us, indifferent to our presence. The horned sheep kept apart, a short distance away atop a small hill. The village had only a cluster of homes, a ticket office for the ferry, and a waiting room with food served.

Johnson and Boswell didn't have the benefit of such comforts. Unlike our brief time on the ferry, Boswell reports that they sailed by moonlight on a rough sea, "often between black and gloomy rocks." After a "tedious sail," and having to be carried ashore for lack of a landing site, they reached what Boswell calls Icolmkill—an anglicization of the Gaelic for "Iona of (Saint) Columba)"—where he found the tower of the cathedral "a picturesque object." He claims they both shared an emotional experience in their presence on "that illustrious island" where barbarians received the "blessings of religion." Although Boswell says, in the end, the island "did not answer my expectations," he reports that it came up to Johnson's.

However, in his own telling of the visit to Iona, Johnson, rather than religious awe, offers precise descriptions of the ecclesiastical structures, such as "The chapel of the nunnery is now used by the inhabitants as a kind of general cow-house, and the bottom is consequently too miry for examination." He is skeptical about the legend that Iona is the burial place of Scottish kings. He does agree that Iona is "remarkably fruitful," and that the monks chose well. However, the people of the island at the time of his visit, in 1773, "are remarkably gross": "The Island, which was once the metropolis of learning and piety, has now no school

for education, nor temple for worship, only two inhabitants that can speak English, and not one that can write or read."

Not so when we visited. The signs were all in English and those people we overheard were quite fluent. The hotel was bustling, the tourism clearly fruitful. The present population of less than 200 appears to be prospering. Although mobile phone reception is varied, wi-fi is available in the two hotels and at several other locations. The people are in touch with the wider world.

Our taxi ride west was a choice to avoid getting up before dawn to catch the early bus to Craignure and then another to Fionnphort. But we took the lengthy two-stage bus trip back and arrived in Tobermory in time for another excellent dinner. A day well spent.

When Johnson and Boswell left Mull and the Western Isles, they made a number of stops on the mainland of Scotland, including a few days at Boswell's family home, before Boswell put Johnson on a coach that carried him back to England, Johnson telling Boswell as he left "that the time he spent in this tour was the pleasantest part of his life." Yet in his account, Johnson writes: "Of these Islands it must be confessed, that they have not many allurements, but to the mere lover of naked nature. The inhabitants are thin, provisions are scarce, and desolation and penury give little pleasure."

Despite it all, perhaps grudgingly, Johnson concludes his book by noting that his "thoughts on national manners, are the thoughts of one who has seen but little." Yet two years later, in 1777, he is quoted by Boswell as making his most famous paean to life in his city: "Why, Sir, you find no man, at all intellectual, who is willing to leave London. No, Sir, when a man is tired of London, he is tired of life; for there is in London all that life can afford."

Johnson, whatever fulsome thanks he gave Boswell, was certainly relieved to be returning to London at the end of their Scottish journey. Boswell quotes him as having declared years before their trip, "Sir, the noblest prospect that a Scotchman ever sees, is the high road that leads him to London."

Back on the mainland from the Hebrides, Johnson does admit that "we passed through a pleasant country to the banks of Loch Lomond," where they visited the home of wealthy Sir James Colquhoun, then owner of most of the islands on the loch—hardly penury. Yet, he complains that the loch disgusts him because, instead of a setting of soft lawns and shady thickets, it endures "uncultivated ruggedness."

By happenstance, Alison and I also experienced a view of Loch Lomond, unexpectedly, on our return to Glasgow. The Caledonian MacBrayne ferry was fifteen minutes late in landing at Oban, enough of a delay for us to miss our train. Unwilling to wait many hours for the next, we let the ferry's purser help arrange for a taxi, linking us with two others, a large man who turned out to be a Scottish rock musician and a young woman who was an obstetrics nurse in Dundee, returning there from a family visit in Tobermory, where she had grown up.

The hour ride took us along the lovely shores of Loch Lomond, which seemed abundantly cultivated and inviting, and we had time to talk. The musician turned out to be a New York Giants football fan, a rabid one ever since seeing the team play in an NFL game in London. He envied us living in New Jersey, home of Giants stadium. It was one of his life's goals to witness a game there. I was unwilling to tell him I'd rather row to Iona than endure that experience.

The nurse was happy to be away from the limitations of Mull, to be living in a city with all a city has to offer, unwilling to ever return to her birthplace. I get that. The repetitions of walking the same few streets, climbing the same hill, patronizing the same row of shops, eating in the same restaurants, looking out at the same views. Yet after a day in what I considered the grim hulk of Glasgow, I missed the colors and the harbor and the sense of open space.

For whatever Johnson's and today's London—or New York or Paris—have to offer, they are not all that life can afford, merely cities. Perhaps it's seeing widely—both on the journey and at the destination—that really matters, the realizations of alternatives, of unexpected possibilities. Perhaps a more accurate statement would be that when one is tired of discovering, one is tired of life.

WALTER CUMMINS has published seven short story collections—*Witness*, *Where We Live*, *Local Music*, *The End of the Circle*, *The Lost Ones*, *Habitat: stories of bent realism*, *Telling Stories: Old and New*. He also has two collections of essays and reviews—*Knowing Writers* and *Death Cancer Madness and Meaning*. More than one hundred of his stories, as well as memoirs, essays, and reviews, have appeared in magazines such as *New Letters*, *Kansas Quarterly*, *Virginia Quarterly Review*, *Under the Sun*, *Arts & Letters*, *Confrontation*, *Bellevue Literary Review*, *Con- necticut Review*, in book collections, and on the Web. With Thomas E. Kennedy, he is founding co-publisher of Serving House Books, an outlet for novels, memoirs, and story, poetry, and essay collections. For more than twenty years, he was editor of *The Literary Review*. He teaches in the graduate writing programs at Fairleigh Dickinson University.

THOMAS E. KENNEDY's many books include novels, story and essay collections, literary criticism, anthologies, and translations. The four novels of the *Copenhagen Quartet* were published by Bloomsbury in the U.S. and the U.K. (*In the Company of Angels*, 2010; *Falling Sideways*, 2011; *Kerrigan in Copenhagen, A Love Story*, 2013; and *Beneath the Neon Egg*, 2014). His two collections from New American Press are *Last Night My Bed a Boat of Whiskey Going Down* (2010) and *Riding the Dog: A Look Back at American* (2008). His stories, essays, travel pieces, interviews, poems, and translations appear regularly in American and European periodicals. His writing has won an O. Henry Award, a Pushcart Prize, a National Magazine Award, a Charles Angoff Award, and other prizes. With Walter Cummins, he is founding co-publisher of Serving House Books.

www.ingramcontent.com/pod-product-compliance
Lightning Source LLC
Chambersburg PA
CBHW070946190726
48292CB00004B/1351

* 9 7 8 1 9 4 7 1 7 5 2 3 5 *